WISDOM

WOODSON
AND NALEIGHNA KAI

This book is a work of nonfiction. These accounts are from the author's perspective and memories, and as such, are represented as accurately and faithfully as possible. To maintain the anonymity of the individuals involved, some of the names and details have been changed.

Wisdom: Blessings from Imperfections
Copyright © 2022 by The Macro Group, LLC All rights reserved.

Edited by J. L. Woodson and Naleighna Kai
naleighnakai@gmail.com
Cover Designed by J. L Woodson: www.woodsoncreativestudio.com
Interior Designed by Lissa Woodson: www.naleighnakai.com
Beta Readers: D. J. Mitchell, Christine Pauls, and Kelsie Maxwell

ISBN 9781952871443 (Trade paperback)
ISBN 9781952871375(E-Book)

Without limiting the rights under copyright reserved above, no part of this publication may be reproduced, stored in, or introduced into a retrieval system, or transmitted, in any form, or by any means (electronic, mechanical, photocopying, recording, or otherwise) without the express written permission of both the copyright owner and the publisher of this book, except in the case of brief quotations embodied in critical articles and reviews. The scanning, uploading, and distribution of this book via the Internet or via any other means without the permission of the owner is illegal and punishable by law. For permission, contact Naleighna Kai at naleighnakai@gmail.com.

The Macro Group, LLC
1507 E. 53rd Street, #858
Chicago, IL 60615

Scripture quotations are taken from the King James Version (KJV), public domain.

DEDICATION

Jean Woodson,
Eric Harold Spears,
LaKecia Janise Woodson,
Mildred E. Williams,
Anthony Johnson,
L. A. Banks,
Octavia Butler,
Tanishia Pearson Jones,
Emmanuel McDavid, and
Priscilla Jackson

J. L. Woodson & Donisha
Shawn Williams, Sesvalah, Ehryck, Janice
La Ammitai, Jamyi Joi, Janine Ingram, and the
members of NK's Tribe Called Success

ACKNOWLEDGEMENTS

Special thanks goes out to: The Creator from whom all Blessings and opportunities flow, Sandy (my true mother), my son, J. L. Woodson (for the awesome cover designs for this Merry Hearts series), Sesvalah, Bettye Odom, Janice M. Allen, Debra J. Mitchell, Royce Slade Morton, Bunny Ervin, J. L. Campbell, Kelly Peterson, Janine A. Ingram, Ehryck F. Gilmore, Betty Clawson, Jamyi Joy, Stephanie M. Freeman, Unique Hiram, Marie L. McKenzie, Shawn Williams, Dr. Vanessa Howard, the Kings of the Castle Ambassadors, Members of Naleighna Kai's Literary Cafe, the members of NK's Tribe Called Success, the members of Namakir Tribe, and to you, my dear readers . . . thank you all for your support.

Much love, peace, and joy,
Naleighna Kai

Naleighna Kai

Sometimes we fall apart only to put the pieces back together in a different way for the road ahead. I met J. L. Woodson and many others two years ago at a time when the world ground to a screeching halt and death seemed to hold sway. But life has a way of bringing light to the darkest places. Never before or since have I met a person that could harness the words flowing from my pen into a single element to give my books their true face. As I look around my office, I smile at his artwork—because that is exactly what it is—adorning the walls.

An artist's life is never an easy one, and the real ones know pain on a level that speaks to your soul. J. L. Woodson is one such artist.

As I edited his book, I had the honor of meeting this talented young man on another level. His bravery and vulnerability rose from the page like heat.

There is a long walk that we all take on that rocky road to adulthood. Along the way, we question everything we know. I think of the baggage we all carry; the expectations, and dreams that we hang our heart on. With every step he took through the bitter snow on that fateful day in Chicago, I saw what he lost, but also what was gained.

Like a snake shedding old skin that no longer fits, he shed the child he was to make room for the man he was destined to be. And while people and circumstances walked away with what he left in his wake, I saw everything that he picked up—Dignity, Self-Respect, and Vision. Every element is an answer to a prayer unspoken.

—Stephanie M. Freeman, *author of* Necessary Evil, Unfinished Business, *and* Nature of the Beast

Accolades from Nikki Giovanni and Mary B. Morrison
Superwoman's Child: Son of a Single Mother

Dear J. L.
"It was great meeting you and your mom. What a wonderful Superwoman's Child tribute to her. You are a wonderful son of Fisk University."
—Ever on the altar,
Nikki Giovanni

The Things I Could Tell You!
"A definite page turner! J. L. Woodson is absolutely inspiring. Word for word, he compels the reader to sit up and take notice."
--Mary B. Morrison, New York Times Bestselling Author

"This bright young author has written a story that hooks you in the prologue, which cleverly describes the intense ending of the story. The story is a pretty accurate portrayal of the effects abuse can have on a family and the extreme results that can occur. We thoroughly enjoyed this story. A Big 'Write On' to J. L. Woodson!"
—Darcina Garrett, The Literary Diversions Book Club

"I strongly encourage parents/adults to read this book because it shows what we, as women, tolerate sometimes for too long."
—R. Hopes

Chapter 1

"You want me to do what?" Noah bolted upright from his resting spot on the exposed root of an olive tree facing the mountains in the East.

A sigh of warm wind stirred the scant hair on Noah's head as the voice of God filled his being. "Build an ark."

Noah sat back and stroked his silver beard. Finding God at the great easel He had made of the sky which always blessed his soul. But the morning was different. Darkness still swathed the land in slumbering whispers. Over the years, waking out of a dead sleep only meant one of two things. Someone had died or God had wanted to talk with him.

"And an ark is …" Noah questioned as he searched the skyline and his surroundings. For what, he couldn't be sure.

The idea of God parking his heavenly body on a neighboring tree stump was almost laughable, but part of Noah half expected to see his Creator basking in the sunlight He created.

"An ark is a boat. A big wide one made of gopher wood with rooms for you, your family, and the animals that you'll take along with you," God answered stirring the leaves above Noah's head as a lone rooster heralded the news that morning had broken."

"And why exactly would we need any kind of boat around these parts?" Noah countered. "We've only seen enough water for flocks and veggies."

"All of that is about to change," God said. "I'm sending a lot of water your way. Flood the earth, so to speak. Wipe things clean and start over."

"That seems a little … harsh." Noah peered over his shoulder, half expecting to get whacked on the head like a disobedient child.

"Drastic times call for drastic measures. Only you and your family are guaranteed to be saved from the devastation."

"What about everyone else?"

"Like I said, only you and your family …"

The sincerity and the finality in God's tone made Noah shudder inwardly before tightening his robe about him. "So, an ark?"

"Yes, about three hundred cubits long, fifty cubits wide, and thirty cubits high." The still small voice sounded distant, as if God were pacing about deep in thought. Noah wondered if his Father in Heaven clasped his hands behind his back while worrying the same strip of clouds like a carpet.

Noah thought of his Heavenly father walking back and forth like a human while gnawing on the end of a pipe, sort of how he and his older brother used to imitate their own earthly father before falling in a heap, breathless with laughter.

"So, we're just killing off random people these days with no chance at redemption?" Noah asked, still laughing at the memory.

"Watch it, Noah. And yes, I know that you don't know what an ark is, but I'll make sure you have the necessary tools to pull it off. And there will be levels to this thing—lower, second and third stories, and add a window up top and a door on the side, too."

"Can't I tell someone? Anyone?"

"Even if you did, there's no turning them away from their wicked ways. I'm done. And I mean done, done. The flood *is* coming, and they haven't heeded my voice before, and trust me when I say you'd better have your hind parts on that ark or—"

"I get it," Noah said with a weary sigh.

One of the olives hidden in the branches above Noah's head thumped against his skull hard enough to hurt. He rubbed the top of his head and peered at the branches. "And what's the deadline for completing this ark?"

"As soon as possible." God said in a tone that could have etched His words in stone. "It's going to rain for forty days and forty nights before you can step foot on dry ground."

"So, I'm nearly six hundred years old and you expect me to build an ark,"—he spread his arms wide—"Yaaaay big in the middle of nothing but sand and sable, for a flood, the likes of which no one has ever seen or ever heard of before." Noah countered before covering his head for fear of another unruly olive bonking him on the head.

"And there's no reason to explain why you're doing this," God said as the wind picked up, making the leaves chatter as some of the birds left for quieter surroundings.

"And that's going to go over real nice."

"And that's my point. It's time to start from scratch," God said as the dog sleeping a few feet away from Noah rolled over on his back as if he were basking in a belly rub. "I'm tired of talking. I can show them better than I can tell them."

Noah scanned the area, taking in the sloping green hills and the smoke from his wife's cooking fire curling up into the early rays of sunlight. All of it would be gone—the hills, their home. The thought alone made him tear up.

"So why am I being spared? Why is my family being spared?" Noah whispered as he thought of his shepherd and his infant son being swept away.

"Because you're living right."

Noah looked up as the sun warmed his face like a father's pride, but then the image of a woman who had been giving him major grief filled his mind.

"Wait a minute," Noah said. "And I don't have to bring my mother-in-law."

"I did say family," God insisted.

"We can't manage to be in the house for forty minutes let alone forty days and forty nights," Noah stood, pacing. The last time that woman was under his roof, she taunted his wife Emzara so much that she fled the dinner table. Rather than follow and apologize, the portly old woman with the mole on her nose scraped her daughter's plate onto her own. "More for me," she said with wild glee.

"Don't be so dramatic," God warned breaking Noah's concentration.

"Have you met her?" Noah snapped

"I made her," God reminded him.

"Then you know *exactly* what I'm talking about." The memory of the woman's flatulence filling the sleeping quarters making his youngest son storm outside to sleep with the livestock filled his mind.

"This will be a test of your faith," God said. Noah could swear a note of concern laced his voice.

"No, it's a test of my patience because if I have a few more run-ins with that woman, the Cain and Able won't be the only well-known family issues," Noah warned as he left the shady spot to trek across the grass.

"See, why do you bring up old things?" God asked before adding a hint of pink to the clouds still bathed in the remains of nightfall.

"Because they are relevant to current things," Noah shot back. "And I'd also like to add that folks already think I'm crazy."

"Let them think whatever they like. Can you feed your family on other people's thoughts?" God snapped. "Can their thoughts save them? I will use whomever and whatever I please on this rock. I made it and I can crack it open like an egg. What do the opinions of man matter to me?"

"None I guess," Noah said eyeing the jug of wine he carried to offer along with the first fruits from the crops.

"Now mind that business that will keep you alive."

"Can we revisit the mother-in-law thing?" Noah asked in the sweetest tone he could manage.

"Give it a rest," God said as a storm of olives fell from the tree in front of Noah.

Chapter 2

By the time the sun covered the valley in warmth and God's good graces, most of the jug of wine warmed Noah's insides and the sack that held the fruit was heavier with the olives he collected. The moment he broached the subject of the ark with his wife he instantly regretted leaving the remainder of the jug on the hill.

"Say what now?" she asked peering into the sack.

"An ark," Noah repeated. "He called it an ark."

She poured the olives into a bowl and sorted them all while giving him the side eye. "For a flood? We don't get rain. Ever. All our water comes from the streams, so is there some rogue wave bubbling up somewhere?"

Noah didn't have an answer for that one.

"So let me get this straight …" She scrubbed the place between her eyebrows before recapping all that he had told her and ending with, "When is all of this supposed to take place?"

"All he said was ... soon," Noah answered with a sheepish grin.

"Soon?" she said returning to sorting the olives. She wrinkled her nose in disgust at one of the green orbs and tossed it into the fireplace and sighed. "This is too farfetched. If you're out there sleeping around with random women just say that. Why bring God into this madness?"

"Yes. I mean of course not. I would never do such a vile thing," Noah said eyeing one of the jugs of wine in the corner. He caught her staring at him and cleared his throat.

"So you're saying it could be in the next few—only a few sunrises away."

"I'm pretty sure He won't let it happen before I'm done building the ark," Noah reassured her taking a step closer to the table.

"It's all this uncertainty for me." She reached over to stir something in the cauldron over the fire. "You do whatever you feel you need to do."

"Well, there's more to it than just building this thing," Noah said wincing at her dismissive tone.

"There's more?" she said tapping the spoon on the edge of the pot. She turned to face him. "Well spit it out."

"We have to bring two of each animal on the ark," Noah said in a rush.

"You're not serious." She sorted the last of the olives into the bowl and popped one in her mouth.

"He is deadly serious." He shook his head. "Ooops. Wrong choice of words there."

She turned and spat the olive pit into her hand before tossing it into the fireplace making the flames crackle in protest. "Let me throw a scenario at you."

"Shoot," he said, easing into a chair

"Two anteaters?" She tossed him an olive.

"Yes." He bit down on the tender flesh and a burst of rich oil sweet and salty filled his mouth. He chewed then threw the pit but missed the flames.

"And two ants?" she threw out. "You see the problem?"

He did, but the fact that she hadn't taken his head off the moment he opened his mouth gave him a false sense of security. Noah had no intentions of pushing the conversation any further. "He will have to sort that out at a later time."

"Do you really believe He is going to wipe everything out?" she asked moving away to stir the pot once more.

"I don't think He would make idle threats," Noah said, staring at the olive pit on the floor.

"And just leave us floating around with a bunch of animals?"

"Let Him tell the story, that's what's already happening. And He means the two-legged animals that walk upright."

...the sons of God saw the daughters of men that they were fair; and they took them wives of all which they chose. —Genesis 6:2

There were giants in the earth in those days; and also after that, when the sons of God came in unto the daughters of men, and they bear children to them, the same became mighty men which were of old, men of renown. —Genesis 6:4

The end of all flesh is come before me; for the earth is filled with violence through them; and behold, I will destroy them with the earth. —Genesis 6:13

"All right. Let me have a talk with my mother," she said before kicking the pit into the flames.

"Yes, we'll tell her we *want* her to come." Noah clasped his hands. "Whatever you think is best. I'll even come if you want."

Emzara gave Noah the side eye. "You know she always does the *opposite* of what you tell her."

"That's the point," Noah said with a toothy grin.

Chapter 3

"So what's that big monstrosity you're building over at your place?"

Noah took a long swig of his drink. "Well, in a few weeks a flood will come and wipe out everything on the face of the earth." Shoot! He didn't mean to say that. The wine must be doing the talking.

"A flood?" a burly bald man said over the rim of his goblet. "What's that?"

Noah tried to cover his mistake, but it sounded strange even to his own ears.

"You are talking nonsense," the man's drinking buddy shouted. The two couldn't have been better matched. The burly man stroked his beard and the thinner man beside him gnawing on a leg of lamb had plenty of hair on his head but no beard. "The libation in my cup makes more sense than you do."

"Give him a goblet for his time. It's all he came in for anyway," someone behind Noah cracked, making the entire room erupt into laughter.

"I can't give you any more information about what's to come." Noah looked around at the men jeering at him and wondered if they would be laughing as the water destroyed their homes, their crops and ultimately their lives. The thought saddened him in no small way.

The man made a shooing motion with his hand. "Now go away you crazy old man."

And God saw that the wickedness of man was great in the earth, and that every imagination of the thoughts of his heart was only evil continually.

And it repented the Lord that he had made man on the earth, and it grieved him at his heart. Genesis 6:5-6

* * *

Come thou and all thy house into the ark; for thee have I seen righteous before me in this generation.

And they that went in, went in male and female of all flesh, as God had commanded him: and the Lord shut him in.

And the rain was upon the earth forty days and forty nights. (Genesis 7:1, 16-17)

Chapter 4

"And every living substance was destroyed which was upon the face of the ground, both man, and cattle, and the creeping things, and the fowl of the heaven; and they were destroyed from the earth: and Noah only remained alive, and they that were with him in the ark." — Genesis 7:23

"That rainbow hung in the sky like a jewel. Do you remember husband? God's promise on a field of blue?"

Emzara glanced at Noah's sleeping form when she didn't receive an answer. The sheets were tangled about his waist and legs as he snored fitfully, oblivious of her looking on.

"Nothing … nothing." He whimpered and jerked in his sleep.

Tears welled in her eyes. She smoothed a hand over the colors she stitched together for his new robe.

"The sounds never left him, Father," she prayed, wiping a tear that slid down her cheek. "The way they pounded on the doors.

The howls and screams. They were louder than the animals in the bowels of your ark. The silence was worse. I don't question. I never do. I just …" She bit down on her bottom lip and looked away from the body of her beloved who was lost to the world on the jug of fig wine she made sure sat by his bedside when the dreams of what transpired were too close.

Why is irrelevant. My ways are not your ways and that is a mercy. Noah is as I fashioned him. I took the foolish, base things of the world to confound the so-called wise.

"But he suffers so, Lord," she whispered and sorrow filled her heart. "He did what you asked. He was shamed and humiliated for following You. No matter what they did or said, he set his face like stone and followed You. And this is his reward? He's a shadow of the man I married. He is …"

Precisely as I made him. You and your children are alive because he followed Me. It is far more important that he remember and that you and your children's children do the same. Tread lightly, child. Humanity hangs in the balance.

"And if I choose not to remember? Then what? Look at him," she countered. "Your love hurts. It costs so much. Can you not see what it has cost him?"

The silence spread between them, and Noah cried out and began to toss and turn. Emzara abandoned her chair and joined her husband on their bed. He snuggled closer before tumbling back into oblivion.

I give you free will, Emzara. But I know the compassion, the empathy I placed inside you and the generations that will follow. Yes, I think you will remember for the same reason you're holding him now.

Her tears flowed hot and free and she wrapped her arms and legs around Noah's body in an attempt to drawn the nightmares from him like a poison. "I don't want him to be alone."

Yes, my child. Just as you held him that fateful night when I erased the world with my tears, you are here to hold him close to remind him that there is good in the world so long as love lives.

"He even cries about my mother not making it onto the ark, and I never thought that would happen in my lifetime." She released a long, weary sigh and settled further into the cloth. "The covenant will hold? That rainbow you sent? You promised not to do this again."

Yes, I said . . . and I will establish my covenant with you, neither shall all flesh be cut off any more by the waters of a flood; neither shall there anymore be a flood to destroy the earth.

Emzara closed her eyes. The last thing she heard was . . .

Sleep child. I will hold you both this night and forever.

Give Up A Year of Your Life

"If you give up a year and finish writing this story, it will change your life forever."

My mother told me many things earlier in my life. This one was spot on. I had written an English assignment that frightened my teacher so badly that she called my mother up to school to have a "conversation" with the principal, the counselor, the police, and two other people. Only for them to find out what I had written was pure fiction. Well, mostly.

At that time, we were living in hiding to protect a woman who had barely escaped death by her husband's hand. My Aunt Vee had tried to leave him before and ended up being unable to walk for four weeks because of what he had done. My mother changed jobs, moved out of the city, changed my school, changed her phone number, disconnected from family members, and other things to make it harder for Aunt Vee to be found.

I remember my mother had driven at top speed, gunning it to the airport because the plans to bring Aunt Vee to Chicago had nearly fallen apart. The airline ticket had been purchased in her "new name" and the ticket agents weren't letting her on the plane in New York. A lot of changes had transpired after that 1995 bombing in Oklahoma. My mother had to get to the airport in Chicago to pay for a new ticket on this end for them to let Aunt Vee on the plane. My mother made a tear-filled plea and people graciously allowed my mother to the head of the line. The airline personnel opened it up early because the New York airport called to tell them what was going on. Aunt Vee was hiding in the airport bathroom in New York while it was all worked out, petrified because the trip her husband was supposed to be on had suddenly been cancelled and he was on his way home. He was sure to track her to the airport if he discovered that she was gone.

Watching my Aunt Vee those weeks after she arrived was the most painful experiences I could recall. She was so afraid of everything. Wouldn't leave the house. And once when I was late coming home from school, she broke down in sobs because she feared that he had found us and had done something to me.

Elements of that experience flowed into those seven pages of my freshman year English homework. The assignment was to create a scary story. Others wrote the *Friday the 13th* or "Jason" kind of stories. I wrote what it would be like to kill one parent to protect another. So yeah, that call had to be made to figure out what the heck was going on in my house.

My mother, a published author just starting out in the industry, read those pages, and was floored. She said, "If you give up a year and finished writing this story, it will change your life forever."

Truer words had never been spoken.

Thinking back on that time in my life, I am reminded of the bible stories I read as a boy. The one that resonates with this experience, was Noah. A simple request, and a stepping out on faith transformed his life and saved humanity in the process. Here was my mother asking me to sacrifice a year of my life and knowing my future hung in the balance. That leap of faith turned seven pages into a future filled with opportunities the likes of which I could scarcely imagine.

I also gave up going on a school trip to Hawaii. I didn't tell my mother because I knew she was in the middle of getting my second book published and would struggle to pull the money together to make the trip happen. She found out anyway and demanded to know, "Why didn't you tell me? I would have cut back on some things."

I told her, "Mom, in a minute, I'll be able to take everyone we know to Hawaii."

She hugged me when I said that.

Two months later we were given a trip to Hawaii from another grandmother/mentor figure who didn't know what had transpired. I had the most amazing time, ate at some wonderful restaurants, met some new people, and also became a minor celebrity on the island because of a stint on stage with a comedian during a luau. But that's another story for another time. I'm simply sharing this to show that I don't feel like I missed out on anything because I embraced my mother's wisdom and forged ahead, working with a prominent editor to write my first book.

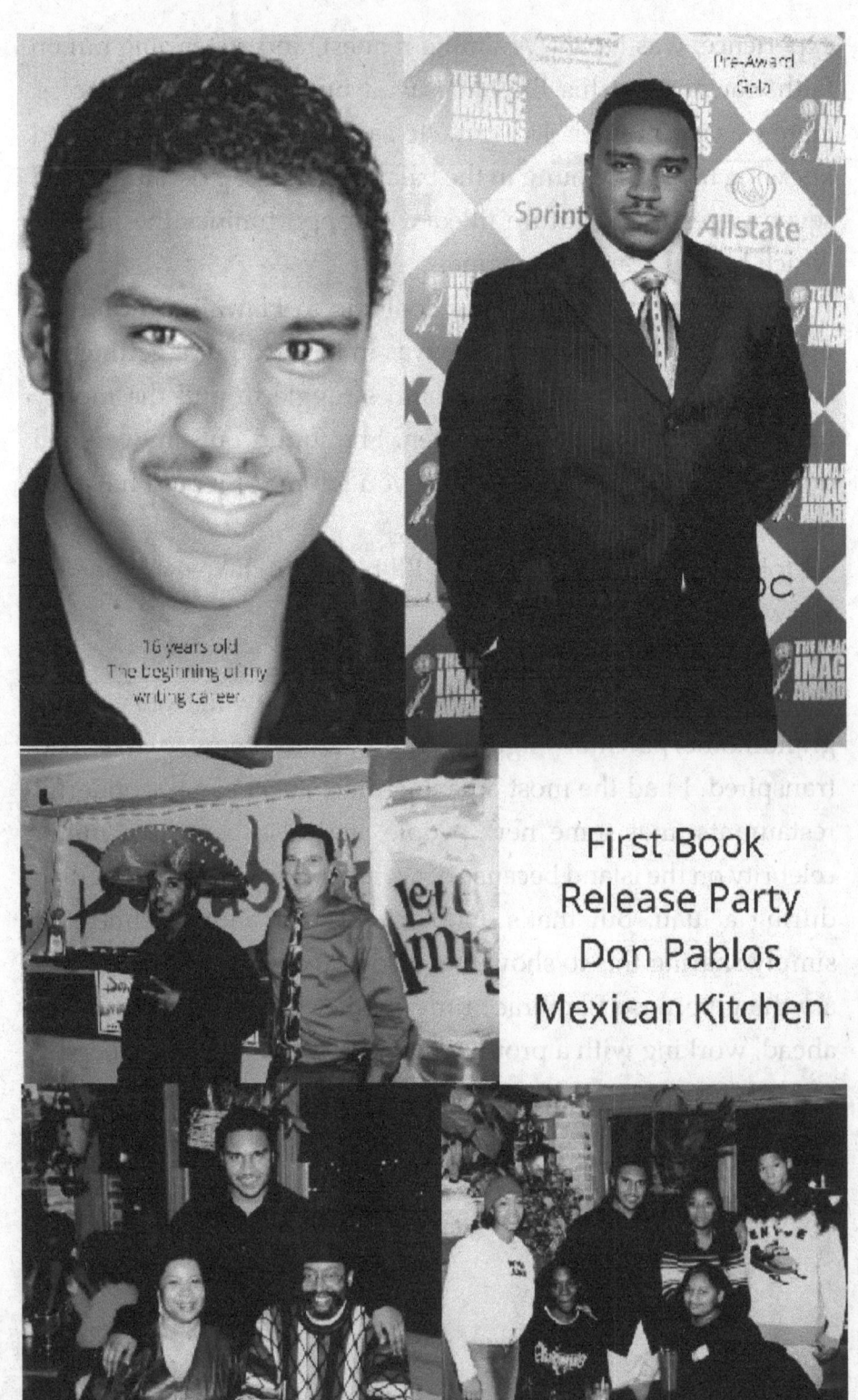

What Had Happened Was...

That change your life part? It didn't come right away.

When my mother moved us from the city to the suburbs, my interest in school slowly took a nosedive. By the time I reached high school, they were threatening to put me in remedial classes. But here's the thing—my standardized test scores were at college level. So why wasn't I performing in anything else (except band and lunch)? And here's the kicker: they secretly tested me three different times and in different locations because they believed I was cheating somehow with the teachers and the counselors watching me. The test scores became higher with each and every test and that seemed to tick them off.

My mother only learned what they were doing when the counselor tried to sell her on placing me into remedial classes. What? A child who was one of only a few fifth graders to be part of the University of Chicago's program for high school students?

A child that was so on top of his game that a public school had to make special accommodations?

Early on, my learning was so advanced that when I transferred to public school for first grade, they had to also switch me to second and third grade classes throughout the day because I needed to be challenged. This ticked off the first-grade teacher so much that she lost her mind and physically assaulted me. The students went to get another teacher, and when Ms. Sweeney arrived to my classroom, she bluntly told Ms. Cleggett, "Ms. Woodson is on her way here. I talked to her and I highly suggest that you not be here when she arrives."

Ms. Cleggett left right then and never returned. That was probably the smartest thing she did that day because my mother ... suffice it to say, she might have needed bail money. The teacher didn't have the patience to deal with youngsters, but she especially did not like me. "Someone even presses his undershirts," she spat at another teacher when she glared at me one day as the class stood in line for gym. She also had said something about my complexion and my soft curly hair. Yes, I was loved and well cared for, and I was a bit of a perfectionist back then, but I didn't deserve her punching me down into the chair the way she did. I wouldn't turn in my work unless it was right and she was "Big Mad." I was in first grade, coming from a preschool that was founded by a husband and wife team, Dr. Crawford, and Eleanor Crawford, who were serious about education and discipline too. They didn't put limits on learning. So early on, the fact that they expected me to excel was already embedded. "I can, I shall, I will" was what I learned from them.

Somewhere along the way, especially when we moved to the burbs, my desire for learning simply ... disappeared. It showed in my work, but not in those test scores.

When my mother came up to the school, she could not understand what was happening. This is where things got ugly. The counselor would not tell her *what* my test scores were. I didn't even know because they wouldn't tell me, so I was already doubting myself. My mom asked several times to see the scores, but he was evasive and said that he couldn't show her. Mom demanded to see the principal and that is where the fact that they'd tested me all those times and never sent a notice home to let her know came out. They were essentially accusing me of being dishonest. … Man, listen … Mom went ballistic. While I wasn't doing what I needed to do in my freshman classes, their plan to put me in classes that were far below my level did not compute. Suffice it to say, those people had never been read up and down in quite the way that my mother did that day. And she didn't use profanity, but the words she did use served the purpose.

Mom immediately pulled me out of that school and under the suggestion from our spiritual leader, she put me into Olive Harvey Middle College (OHMC). This school for high schoolers was housed in the campus of a college. Helen Hawkins, an amazing woman, and even more amazing principal changed my life. She took it back to basics like making me understand and say one thing when I looked in the mirror: "I'm a changed man who takes care of his responsibilities. I am a leader. I am a scholar."

Then Ms. Hawkins showed me the finish line and my life changed even more.

Scholar with a Dollar

"If you're early, you're on time. If you're on time, you're late."

In this school, I had a new look and a new understanding of the term *Scholar*. It wasn't just meant for the students at Harvard or other prestigious institutions. The word was something that could be a projection of a mindset if it's shaped that way. No one grows up thinking they're a thug, but if someone shapes that person's mindset and projects that onto a person, then that's all they will believe they are.

During my time at OHMC, I learned to love and appreciate education again, because one thing they made us understand was that learning happens regardless of those four walls. I can't necessarily say that I understood that while attending that other school. I can't say that I believe the teachers cared at the other school. Every day there was just a waiting game—waiting for the time to go to lunch, band, and home. The only teacher who did care whether I passed or failed was my band teacher. Therefore, that was the only class and activity I cared about. But at OHMC, every teacher all the way down to the basketball coach cared about our future. Life and death is in the power of the tongue, and *Scholar* is the word that Mrs. Hawkins and the teachers at OHMC chose to speak into us. Regardless of our past, regardless of what we had not accomplished education-wise before then, regardless of what side of town we were from …we were, and still are, Scholars.

Here's another way that OHMC differed. Not only was the game plan laid out, but we were given the tools to *envision* and *execute* it. That's when it starts to become something within reach, a feeling more tangible than an apple in your hand. I never envisioned myself going to college before that, but Mrs. Hawkins had a way of making us see the finish line and believe that we could cross it because we knew how to put in that work.

I will tell any parent that has a young one who is getting discouraged with school, show them the finish line of the next part of their learning experience. That is what shifted me out of feeling that school was just something to do until I turned 18 and was able to be out on my own.

The college tour took me to witness HBCUs up close and personal. There, I saw people who looked like me doing great things. On the way to becoming adults who were equipped for careers or entrepreneurship.

I wanted to get away from Chicago. It wasn't that I didn't love my mother, but an eagerness to explore other places had settled in my soul. Now all Superwoman could do was reflect and say the three famous and embarrassing *Oh Boy* statements. "Oh Boy, I remember when you were little." Or "Oh, boy, shut up! I was there to wipe, your little thing." Or the all-time favorite, "Oh, boy, I was the one in labor with you, and you didn't even want to come out with your complicated behind." She was in labor for twenty-six hours and they had to keep coming through to shake her stomach because I was asleep and refusing to make an entrance. Then thirty minutes after they threatened to go in and get me, the doctor checked up under the hood and said, "It's show time!"

Getting out of Chicago was the best part of the tour because I hadn't done or seen much outside of the area. I think the best parts about the college tours was learning the history behind the colleges and universities, from what transpired back in earlier times to how it affects us today. I definitely appreciate that the colleges Ms. Hawkins selected for the tour were important because they held a piece of my past—our past—within those walls.

College life introduced us to people who were very into African American culture and history, and also people who were all about fraternity life. Sisters who were all about Black Power back then are now some of those same ones who are at the forefront of Black Lives Matter.

On the Fisk campus, we walked down halls lined with murals by Aaron Douglas, an American painter, illustrator, and visual arts educator who was a major player in the major Harlem Renaissance. His life is amazing because it's well preserved in the building and in the history of the school. They don't let anyone forget about him and his purpose.

The colleges I found more alluring were Fisk, Alabama A&M, and Tuskegee.

I considered Tennessee State, but that place was a maze. I got lost on our tour just from making a quick trip to the bathroom. One thing was certain, if I would've attended either Alabama A&M or Tennessee State, I would never have had an issue with weight gain because of all the walking it took to get from class to class.

We also visited the Birmingham Civil Rights Institute and 16th Street Baptist Church in Birmingham, Alabama, the church that had been bombed by white supremacists, killing four Black girls: Addie Mae Collins, Cynthia Wesley, Carole Robertson, and Carol Denise McNair. We also went to Clark Atlanta, Morris Brown, Spelman, Morehouse and then to the Martin Luther King Memorial. All have significant ties to history.

Sometimes the tour guide truly made the school interesting by sharing what they knew and how they felt about the school. This is where I learned that first impressions were extremely important. One tour guide at Morehouse was condescending and turned me off with his dismissive attitude of "You'll be here if you want to be here." I wasn't the only one who felt like he didn't care whether we were informed about the school or its importance. Morehouse has produced some amazing young men who have made significant contributions to the world. If there had been someone else as the tour guide, I have a feeling I might have considered that college as one of my top picks right along with Fisk University. One of the major things that stood out about Fisk was our tour guide, Fitzgerald Heslop. "If you are able to walk these halls, and attend the classes, know this, you didn't *choose* Fisk. Fisk chose you." There was so much pride in just that statement and the way he said it. He made it sound like becoming a Fisk scholar was a higher calling.

On the second tour, we went to the University of Arkansas, Pine Bluff, Mississippi Valley, Mississippi State, Mississippi Valley State University, and Xavier in New Orleans.

I believe the experience would have been more complete if we were able to have a simulated class scenario at the schools. We didn't get a chance to see the classes. I wish more college tours gave us a glimpse of the inside of the class so we could get a feel for things other than just the buildings, sleeping quarters, and structures that had historical significance. While I do think that gaining understanding of why the building had been constructed and who it's named after is important, in my mind, I was like, "That's cool and all, but what are we getting into while we're here?"

Every time I watch the opening credits to the television show, *Queen Sugar*, I think about the OHMC HBCU College Tour. The scene reminds me of the time when I was on that coach bus, looking out the window on the way to different campuses. Some of those schools were surrounded by farmlands and rural areas. You can feel the history. You can feel that legacy lives here. At that time I wondered … what legacy would I leave on this earth.

Write the Book …
It Will Change Your Life

When it comes to my unexpected writing career, in my honest opinion, I've treated it like the line from *Field of Dreams*, "If you build it, they will come." That goes all the way back to the origins of my first book, *The Things I Could Tell You,* which sprang from a creative writing assignment for English class. My Mother and teachers read those seven pages and saw that talent in me. When she told me I should expand that story into a book, I literally just said, "Okay."

So when another opportunity came from *New York Times* Bestselling author, Zane, to write a short story in the *Breaking the Cycle* anthology, all I needed to do was produce. When it comes to writing or really anything creative, money might be the reward or the result from having a great product, but that has never been my focus. And that goes double for contracts, awards, or accolades that may come as well, making that the reason I put pen to paper taints my view of the project. I focus on the project itself. I focus on the purpose and the message. Those are the things that are the most important. Words on a page can change lives. Sharing challenges and triumphs can also help people through the times they might have similar experiences.

Writing that short story, "God Does Answer Prayers," was perhaps the most organic feeling I've had in my literary career. Although the deadline was shortened because of a miscommunication, which meant staying up all night to produce the piece, the story felt real. I cried while writing because I imagined that it was something happening to me (although I had never personally experienced what was on the page). I let my mind take over and let my fingers freely type the words. Next thing I knew, I was finished. The outcome was that the anthology won the 2006 NAACP Image Award for Outstanding Fiction. The best part was receiving a book deal with an imprint of Simon & Schuster. However, what was even more rewarding, was receiving email and Facebook messages from people who said my short story really touched them.

My second book *Superwoman's Child: Son of a Single Mother* was published by a traditional publishing house. I remember the support and love I received from everyone when it was released. Encouraging words came from established authors, and I was able to travel all over the country for book signings and speaking engagements. I was grateful to Zane for the opportunity. The rewards and the experiences that came with it were priceless. Like being able to present an award to Octavia Butler during a Book Expo America Convention and being able to hang with *New*

York Times Bestselling and National Bestselling Authors such as Mary B. Morrison, Kimberla Lawson Roby, Mary Monroe, L. A. Banks and so many others.

The biggest reward of all was being nominated for an NAACP Image Award for Outstanding Literature for 2007, the 38th year of the award. I consider myself a modest person, so when my mother told me the news, on the outside it may have seemed that she was more excited than I was. On the inside, after I took it all in, I was doing cartwheels and backflips. The awards were not the reason the fiction piece based on several of my life experiences was written, but the fact that it was so well-received did make me proud.

The magnitude of the accomplishment didn't officially hit me until I was in Los Angeles and on the red carpet with my Mom. The trip was my first time in California, and I just loved being there. Warm weather, palm trees and events surrounding the awards show were an awesome combination. The pre-award show gala was awesome, and I was dressed to impress with a suit that had to be altered by my Godmother, Linda Belton, without me being there. With classes in full swing, I couldn't leave Nashville to come to Chicago first, so my flight went straight to Los Angeles. It was hard to stay calm and collected when people I've seen in some of my favorite movies and television shows were all in the same room. I had the camera ready, and looking back, I'm glad my pride didn't get in the way of seizing some great moments. I took photos with Michael B. Jordan, Michael K. Williams, Brian White, Kadeem Hardison. I met and hugged Rain Pryor, shook hands with Judge Mathis and was able to see Prince on stage.

One of the Saturday events was the FedEx Golf Challenge. First time I've ever played the sport and with a few quick lessons from a youngster who was considered and rising star in the world of golf, I came in second place!

That night, I remember finally seeing in the program who I was in a category with, and thinking to myself, "Wow, your name is with Hill Harper. That's pretty dope." Even though we arrived two hours early, that red carpet experience took a while. I think my mother knew that the chances of winning wasn't high, so she didn't rush me through. She watched the people ahead of us and saw that they had publicists and others to "announce" their presence. When it was my turn to hit the carpet in front of what seemed like a hundred cameras, my mother stepped forward, lifted her chin, and said, "Introducing, J. L. Woodson, Nominated for Outstanding Literature for his book, *Superwoman's Child: Son of a Single Mother*." Then she slid off to the other side to allow the cameramen and journalists to snap their photos.

During the session, one of them said, "You have an *amazing* publicist." It took me a minute to understand who they were talking about. Honestly, I have to share that it was a palm-to-head slap moment because I didn't understand the game. I scanned the crowd and said, "That's not my publicist, that's my Mama!" Everyone laughed because she had this look on her face that said, "Darn it, young man. I'm busted."

They held up the line because they asked my mother to come back onto the carpet with me so they could take pictures of us together. Fun times. When we finally made it inside, my category had already been awarded and my mother said, "Hill Harper won." And for a split second, that hope that I held flickered out, but it was instantly ignited again when I leaned over to whisper to my Mom, "But I loved that red carpet though." She gave me the biggest smile as she chuckled.

I may not have won the award that night, but just to be nominated in the same category as Hill Harper, to be there in that space and share that experience with my mother, I didn't feel like someone who had lost something valuable. I wouldn't have traded that experience for anything in the world.

Some mothers have this certain kind of magic, this knowing look about them steeped in oceans of love. When the doctors place their newborn in their arms, the pain, the hours, and that gunk all over the baby's body just disappears. Well, at least until you get older and they recount the tale of your birth and the eternity it took to get you there, but I digress. Two lives change in the moment: yours and theirs.

When a mother looks at that brand new human being, I think *our* lives flash before their eyes. They glimpse a million splendid futures, each more brilliant than the sun, and a path that crackles and hums like the rhythm of the earth. And maybe fate or faith adds a detour or a billion. Moms know. They see your potential, believe in it so strongly that anything else is fantasy.

Thank you, Mom, for your faith in me.

Sweat Equity

She said:

My son continues to inspire me because his comeback story is nothing short of amazing. He didn't manage to pull the straight A's needed to maintain that scholarship to Fisk, but I expected him to try. Math and science were always tough subjects for him, but it was learning to juggle so many things, including becoming a member of a fraternity that helped to broaden his experiences. He learned a series of lessons that helped fashion him into a man who believes that God has his back.

  A year after having to leave Fisk and go into the work force to regroup, his job in Nashville ended and he was forced to make the trek back home to Chicago and to another series of lessons. That wonderful lakeview apartment he had faith to claim on my behalf and then shifted me into before he left for that freshman year became a little "too tight" for me and this young man who was always about handling his business. And for a moment, in my mind, he wasn't making himself the priority. Everything and everyone came before him.

Well, mama did what she felt best at the time and shook up the nest. Having an "address" became paramount after I "ushered" him out of my house — which meant *he* instantly became his first priority — as it should be. Finishing what he started—getting that degree, getting to that place where he could sustain himself became his focus whether I was here to experience it or on the Spirit side watching over him.

* * *

He said:

Moving back home after losing everything was hard, but my time in Nashville had run its course. No job, no school, back in my mother's house again was a lot to handle, but I thought I was dealing with it by pushing forward and putting on a smile as though everything was all right. During that time, no one ever really talked about depression when it came to Black people. We press forward as if the cares of the world aren't weighing heavily on our shoulders. I didn't have any insurance to talk to a professional, even if I had identified the issue. In hindsight I was depressed but didn't know it at the time. My mother must have picked up on something because she watched my actions, more than listening to my words.

The most difficult part was being in this new territory of having to find a job when jobs were scarce. This was during the recession and slightly after. I'm used to working and making my own way, so hearing rejections or companies saying that the job was filled months ago was disheartening. Even people I had on the inside at some companies said there was a hiring freeze. I stayed up overnight submitting applications, cover letters, and resumes and going down a "YouTube Learning" rabbit hole. When I saw the sun rising, that's when I knew it was time to get a few hours of sleep. I was thoroughly knocked out.

This point in my life, I felt like all was lost and couldn't see that my new beginning was right around the corner.

What my mother saw was that I was sleeping during the day. She didn't realize that I had been up working and searching for opportunities and a new place to live through the night. I didn't communicate that to her, but she felt I wasn't holding up my end of things when it came to finding a job and a new place and also putting in that "Sweat Equity" on doing the things I was supposed to do around the house.

On her birthday, my mother packed my things and had them waiting for me when I returned home. She said, "You can either take the items I packed, or you can come back and swing through with a truck and take it all at once. Your choice."

The night my mother "shook the nest," I was at a loss for words because I was already trying to balance the emotions, that came from receiving rejections and feeling like I couldn't do anything. My focus was finding work, not just for the money, but to also feel like a normal adult again. This happened during one of the worst snowstorms Chicago had seen in decades. Everything was shut down. Cars were stranded on Lake Shore Drive. Buses weren't running and Uber wasn't a thing yet. And there I was with a few full suitcases and a box or two, hauling it down 67th Street, late at night.

The only person who was up at the time was my friend Natura. I explained the situation and asked her if I could stay with her. I am grateful she agreed to let me crash there, however the walk from 67th and Oglesby to 43rd and King Drive during a snowstorm where Chicago was blanketed in snow that was thigh high, was a beast.

I lost a lot of my belongings along the way. Watching people walk away with my things was difficult, but I just couldn't carry it all. That thirty-block walk took forever in the cold and snow, but I made it.

A few weeks later, I was placed at a few companies as a contractor and things were finally looking up. I was still actively looking for full-time employment and an apartment to call my own, but being a contractor made it hard to secure a place, especially during a recession where wages were low and long stretches of employment weren't attainable with me moving from company to company.

I don't remember where I saw the ad, it could've been on Craig's list, but after searching high and low for an apartment I could afford, a one-bedroom apartment in the South Shore area became available. I absolutely fell in love with it. This rented-out condo on 73rd and South Shore drive was on the top floor, with a beautiful westward view of Chicago. I really wanted this apartment. The location was great. The rent was around $700-ish. With Lake Michigan as my backyard, how could I not love it? Now all I had to do was get through the application process. The only thing I kept visualizing was me being in that apartment. I could see how I was going to arrange furniture I didn't even own yet. I saw myself inviting my friends over for get togethers.

I didn't necessarily meet all of the criteria for the apartment, and I will admit that I was discouraged while applying. Then I thought "What the heck? I've gotten a lot of things in my life I didn't meet the criteria for. I filled out the application, paid the fees and the first and last month's rent, and before I knew it, I had the keys. Looking back at it now. I chuckle because I'm sure other people applying for that same apartment would be deemed more qualified, but God has a way of working things out. Was it hard? Absolutely! Was it worth it? 1000% Yes!

Reflecting on that forty-plus block walk through the snow, Noah had to travel lighter on the path to his destiny which meant he would lose things along the way. He had a long walk between stepping out on faith and closing the door on the ark. He lost friends, faced ridicule, but he had to leave all of that behind for the bigger journey he would embark on.

Like Noah, I had to walk things out and learn to rely on the skills that my mother and the wise people in my life taught me. Had to embrace the strength and the courage I didn't know that I had.

She said:

Months later, my son was still a little angry with me. My actions on "shifting him out of the nest" had caused the first rift ever in our relationship. I felt really saddened by it, but as a mother, I was afraid of enabling him to a point where he did not reach his full potential. He seemed to have lost that drive he had when he left for Fisk, that spark that signaled that everything was possible. I watched as my mother enabled my brother and helped him hide assets and other things that kept him from being responsible. I did not want to be my mother. I knew my son had more in him than what I was seeing when he came back home. He seemed stagnant and I didn't understand what was truly going on with him. He didn't talk about it and I didn't think to ask. I didn't know what questions to ask.

My birthday present to myself was that I wanted peace of mind, and that meant giving him a hard nudge in the right direction. So, while it hurt, I truly believed I did the right thing.

Interestingly enough, I was the one to give my son a housewarming for his new apartment that he managed to snag within a mere two months of being shaken out of the nest. All of a sudden, between school, the part-time job, paying the bills, and having very little money left over, I believe the message finally sank in—he needed to get his butt back in school, needed to handle his business and get more in line with what he wanted to do: teach, have a wife, children, a home—a life.

That fall, I hired my son to be the disc jockey for the Cavalcade of Authors, a literary event that I give each year in Chicago. While he was on the turntables, a man walked in with Betty Clawson, one of the sponsors of the Cavalcade events. I recognized him immediately as the man in a picture that my son took on the college tour many years ago. This was the only other person who my son handed a copy of his book to while on the tour. The first had been given to the admissions director at Fisk, who invited my son to speak for the Talented Tenth event and then awarded him that Presidential Scholarship. The second book was handed to the man who was the admissions director for Alabama A&M, another one of the schools on that five-city Southern college tour. He had since moved on to become the admissions director for South Carolina State University. But he did not forget my son.

As the two embraced, I said to him, "My son would really like to go back to school."

The man whipped out a business card and placed it in my son's hand. That next week, my son was on top of everything needed to apply. Two months later, he was on a plane to South Carolina and enrolled in the university there. A few months after the unexpected encounter, that admissions director took a job elsewhere, but my son remained, landing a scholarship every semester after that first one. The latest merit scholarship covered tuition, a meal plan, and books. The year before he was scheduled to finish, the school ran into major accreditation issues.

When writing this book, my son called and said, "Mom, do you really want me to put this part in? I don't want people to hate you."

This is the second time he has asked my permission to share a tough part of our lives that might not put me in the best light. He was more concerned about how others would perceive me, than about sharing his truth. Both times, I encouraged him to, "Share your truth, son. This is your story, and people need to read it. Parents will understand what I did and why." I love him for looking out for me, though. In writing inspirational books such as this, it serves no purpose if we can't be vulnerable. And in all transparency, when I read this part of his story, I cried because I didn't know that he lost things along the way to his friend's house. If I had to do it over, I would still have shaken the nest, it just wouldn't have been on that particular day. I think that if he had a chance to do it all over again, he would have communicated his progress rather than let me assume that he was sinking into despair and not making any progress on meeting my deadlines for having his own place.

If there is one thing that I love about being a mother, it's that my son teaches me in words and deeds about exercising my faith muscle. And sometimes, in words and deeds, it is our job to help them remember about exercising their own.

South Carolina State

He said:

The decision to attend South Carolina State University wasn't the easiest one at the time because I had *just* moved to my apartment, *just* had a housewarming, and had finally become settled. I was finding my way. But three things caused me to embrace the change. 1) I would be able to go back to school and finish my degree, and 2) moving to another state would give me a different life experience, 3) by the time I paid rent and all the bills, the only thing left in my pockets were lint and memories. I sold my new furniture, packed up everything I was shipping or taking with me, and stayed with my friend Allie until it was time to leave. The final weeks of being in Chicago during the winter were confirmation that I made the right decision to move to warmer pastures.

While heading to the airport, that freezing cold was nothing nice. I wore a black leather jacket with a grey hoodie under it, and a t-shirt and thermal under that. I had blue jeans with thermal bottoms, insulated boots, hat, gloves, and scarf. On the plane, I was burning up and started peeling off the layers. On that long flight to Columbia, South Carolina, I dripped a bucket of sweat. The walk through Columbia Metropolitan Airport was a culture shock. I felt out of place. This was my first time laying eyes on the place. Things had progressed so quickly that I didn't have enough time to visit SCSU before then. A lot of people were looking at me like I was weird. I mean, I would too if I saw someone walking through the airport with full Chicago winter gear on when it was 75 plus degree weather outside, with the palm trees blowing in the breeze and the sun shining so brightly it looked like a screensaver image.

Of course I didn't know how everything was going to unfold, but the alternative was to stay in Chicago and potentially not progress in life. Although I was there to continue my education, I think this was God's way of shifting me more out of my comfort zone ... again. I did say to myself that I didn't want to be in one place my whole life. Chicago will always be home, but there is plenty more world to take in.

* * *

She said:

Sometimes as parents we worry when our children make life-altering decisions. In his last year of college, my son received a heads-up that the school's finances were questionable, and its accreditation was in trouble.

Choice #1: Return to the school for his senior year, with all the housing and scholarships that were already in place, and hope that the school would ride out a storm that had been building for years.

Choice #2: Give up everything and return to Chicago, enroll in Columbia College with no scholarship in the offing because of the late enrollment, *and* do the one thing he had no intention of doing—move back in with me after plainly saying, "Mom, the next time we'll have to live together is when I need to take care of you." *Now, that's grown man talk right there.*

Life happens, and we have to make detours and adjustments. So he did.

Someone posted articles regarding my son's former school. *The governor is trying to shut it down to force the school to reorganize and get its finances in order.* Well, they'd been in trouble for a minute, and even if they tried to keep it business as usual, the announcement that the school *could* close at any time would be enough to stall enrollment for the next semesters and *that* would devastate the efforts for the school's comeback.

Truthfully, because the scholarships and the working relationships my son had developed down there would make his final stretch of getting his degree an easier one, I wanted him to take that chance and try to finish down there in South Carolina. I kept my opinion to myself. But he thought it through, weighed all sides of the issue, especially the loss of scholarship funds, and went in a more certain direction rather than hanging his hat on an unsure thing—even with all the perks intact. Well, that unsure thing was even more uncertain and it was being played back and forth in the news, which validated his choice; making me glad that I stayed out of trying to push him to go for the money in hand. Because at the moment, that money/scholarship wouldn't be worth a hill of beans if the school lost its accreditation and all he had accomplished there went south.

The score was tied. Grown man, making grown man decisions–1 point. Mom staying out of Grown man's business—1 point.

Go For It!

"It's 4:27AM and J. Cole's "Intro" from 2014 Forest Hills Drive has been on repeat. The song, even though it is short, is very inspiring. It's a song I reflect to. There's a line in there that begins with,

Life gets hard,
You eat your soul
and it ends with, *Look how far I done come*

That part gets to me, because although I still have much to learn, and a lot more living to do. I reflect a lot on where I've been.

Back in 2015, I was listening to this song while bike riding through Chicago's Pullman neighborhood. In a dark place because I was at odds with what I wanted to do with my life and my career. I wasn't happy with the direction it was going in. Then I came across these three words in a sculpture in the center of a square in that historic area: "Go For It". I immediately hit the brakes. Those words were definitely a sign. I sat there for about thirty minutes and didn't say anything. Simply sat in the space and absorbed whatever positive energy was there.

The dark place that I was in seemed to have some light coming in. There I was an English Education Major, knowing deep in my heart that if I continued doing something that I didn't love, doing it just for the sake of money and "security", that it would possibly kill me. My heart was drawn to the freedom that I know as Art—Graphic Design, Videography, Photography to be exact.

Like I said, it was a sign. Being in that space was all it took for me to register at Columbia College, after I had already fully registered for classes at South Carolina State and was a small portion away from graduating there. I switched my major to Graphic Design to finish my senior year at Columbia College in Chicago at a greater cost to me.

Now, whenever I come home, I drive to that same spot, and it's like visiting an old friend. I always seem to leave with a smile on my face, more inspired to go after life. I'm going after better. I'm going after positive changes within. I'm going after all the awesomeness the Universe has in store for me.

Several times in my life, I had to make a choice between two or more things or make a decision and rely on faith and not by sight. Noah had to do the same thing in believing that God would prepare him for the new challenges and beginnings ahead.

The fact that education has had many turns from one level to the next, but the detours all managed to get me to a better place in life. That is how God works.

* * *

After deciding to stay home, I enrolled in Columbia College Chicago. Don't get me wrong, I missed being at South Carolina State. I had just gotten into my stride there. I mainly missed my teachers, friends, and the Fine Arts Department. However, with everything going on and accreditation being in limbo, I just couldn't chance it. That was too long of a drive, just to have to come all the way back if things didn't pan out.

I was already enrolled as an English Education major at SCSU but being heavily involved in the design program and events and always being in the Fine Arts Building, I knew my heart wasn't in teaching English. My only issue now was how could I switch over to Graphic Design as a major. I had a lot of credits for my English Education major. It would take a lot more time to graduate if I switched now. I explained to my advisor that I wanted to change my major, however she confirmed that it would be a waste of time and money to switch now. She advised me to just stick it out.

I'm not going to lie and say that I wasn't disappointed, but I just kept thinking, "As long as I graduate, that's what matters." I ventured into English Education because I wanted to help children who were at a disadvantage in Chicago. I saw what my teachers and Mrs. Hawkins did for me and others at OHMC. I just wanted to continue that progression. I could only imagine what that would be like if we were able to reach children at a younger age. However, having friends and a girlfriend who were already teachers in the Chicago Public School system, I literally saw the life drained from them. I witnessed the stress of having to deal with politics and some parents who believe it's up to the teacher to be the parent 24/7. I literally did not see that for my life.

I sat down and thought about what made me happy. Of course, teaching was fun, but I was less stressed and very inspired when I was thinking about designs and exploring my creativity. Also, who was to say I couldn't still teach or mentor children? I felt stuck because of what my advisor said.

That all changed during the summer, when I went to enroll in summer classes at Harold Washington College. I met with an advisor there to make sure the classes I was going to take, would transfer over to Columbia. She looked over my transcript and saw all the design courses I had taken and asked if I was in Design as a minor. I explained what I wanted to do and what my advisor at Columbia said. She took a few minutes to glance over my transcripts. Looking me in the eye, she told me, "You can change your major and still graduate, in the same timeframe if you take a couple of extra summer school classes." She mapped it out for me on my transcripts and made sure the summer school classes would transfer over.

I registered for my classes and ran down to Columbia to meet with the advisor. I told her flat out, "I'm changing my major." She gave me the same speech about why doing so was a bad idea. I showed her the game plan that was given to me. She looked it over and did not disagree with any part of that plan. I changed my major to Graphic Design that day. I believe God paired me with the advisor from Harold Washington College, right when I needed it.

One day, I had a conversation on a balcony with my cousin Hiram, mentioning the fact that I didn't graduate on time. He said, "You graduate when you are supposed to graduate. If that's two years or four years past the original four years, then that's it."

I may not have graduated from college according to my original schedule but graduating with a degree in a profession that I no longer wanted to be in would have been truly a waste. I look at it like this: it just took me longer to realize what I wanted to do… for me.

That stuck with me even when I was sitting in the auditorium at Roosevelt University with my cap and gown on with all of the other graduates and my family in the other sections. It was a "Lit" graduation. We had awesome music instead of the regular "Pomp and Circumstance." I loved that Columbia allowed us to be ourselves—within reason. We could have fun. So, when I went up to get my degree, instead of just waving at the camera, I doubled-back and gave a head nod to everybody. I still go back and laugh at that clip on YouTube. That night was the end of an awesome chapter in my life, but one thing I learned even from Mrs. Hawkins and Mr. Reynolds is that learning and education never stop, no matter how old we get.

We are lifelong learners.

Honor Thy Father

"Honor thy Mother" was the easy part. She was always there — my rock, my inspiration, my voice of reason.

But "Honor thy Father," a father who had, at best, dipped in and out of my twenty-three years, was the equivalent of pulling an eighteen-wheeler uphill with my front teeth.

How do I honor someone who was never around?

When I was a child, my dad would pop by every now and then. And I enjoyed what little time we spent together. I remember seeing him most when I was in seventh grade. The moments he taught me about football or when he came to a couple of my karate tournaments were firmly etched in my mind. Then one day, he just disappeared. Vanished.

When I was 19, I was hoping to see him at a hearing in child support court for college tuition and other related expenses. He walked right past me, ducked into a restroom, and hid there for more than thirty minutes. He wouldn't — or couldn't — bring himself to see his own son. *What did I do?*

Then a single question from my girlfriend at the time, changed my whole perspective.

"If we get married one day," she asked, "would you invite your dad?"

I started thinking. *Would I?*

The next day, I stared at the phone on my desk for a good fifteen minutes. The time to talk and clear the air had come. I deserved answers. *Why did he walk away? Was it something I did? Did he still (or ever) love me?*

I love my mother. She has been my role model, there for me at every turn. She helped me through high school, encouraged me to start a writing career at fifteen years old, helped me get into college, helped me learn to love God and myself.

Sometimes children—just like adults—focus on what's missing rather than giving thanks for what they have. And I missed having a dad.

The past was spilling into the present: *as a child, his father abandoned him.* What happened to me might someday impact the relationship I have with my future children. I didn't want it to be that way.

The fact that his father had left him should have served as a lesson, not a template, for his life or mine. That father-son bond had to be forged—even late in the game. It was time to break the cycle.

I listened to God, that small voice that whispered, "Don't wait for him. You can be the one to take that first step."

I dialed. On the first try, I got voicemail and left a message. A few days went by and, disappointed, I tried again.

Voicemail. I left another message. My apprehension turned into persistence. I had opened the door and refused to let it swing shut.

Fifteen minutes after that second call, my cell rang. I grabbed it, left my desk at work, and ran to the nearest stairwell. Hearing my father's voice opened the floodgates. Warm tears of happiness streamed down my face.

The next weekend—my birthday week—we met and talked. And talked some more. We talked about our similarities and our relationships with God. He told me why he left: child support issues and his frustration with my mother—who was only seventeen to his twenty-five when they dated—got in the way.

He brought me up to speed on the Mexican side (his side) of the family. We laughed a lot, but we got real. My father answered the questions I'd asked myself for years. He admitted that he should never have taken out his anger with my mom by leaving me.

In our talk, something happened. Something definitely changed in me. All the anger I felt toward him vanished. God placed it in my heart to forgive him.

Eventually, I told him about the time I drove home from Nashville and sat outside of his house wondering if I should ring the bell. He responded by telling me that a drive from Florida to Chicago took him through Nashville, but he didn't have a way to reach me and sadly, didn't know if he should.

I am one of the millions of young people who want to connect with their fathers, but stubbornness and anger often get in the way. My father is one of many who want relationships with their children, but fear, embarrassment or pride keeps them from reaching out. I'm glad that we bridged that gap.

He's not the perfect dad—but who is? I was just glad he was receptive when I contacted him. We talk often and are still in the rebuilding process. We are getting our lives right with each other, but we're also getting right with God.

Honor thy Father and thy Mother? It *can* happen. Sometimes all it takes is for one person to open the door. God will do the rest.

And honestly, sometimes it doesn't work out the way you want it to, it works out the way that it needs to. My father didn't realize that his continued absence gave me the gift understanding a long "goodbye" Sometimes, someone has to leave in order for God to fill that space with much more. I know I did my part—reaching out to him and forgiving him. That is moving in wisdom.

The Prodigal Son

After returning home to Chicago to finish my Graphic Design Degree at Columbia College, I reconnected with my father's side of the family and a place inside of my heart began to heal.

The estranged relationship with my father had everything to do with how I had handled the rest of the Vidal family. I've always thought about them, but I just didn't want to run into my father at any gatherings. I paid a hefty price for it and still have regrets even today.

In my eyes, Aunt Monica was pretty much the super glue of the Vidal side of my family. She'd always made sure to keep up with me when I was a child. I never felt like an outsider, but the more my father abandoned me, the fewer dealings I had with his family.

Once I had the presence of mind to search for them on social media but had difficulty because I had forgotten that a couple of my cousins had last names other than Vidal. I finally found them, though. My cousin Lisa immediately invited me to her daughter's birthday party. I showed up, excited to see this part of my family that I hadn't laid eyes on in a long time.

I was also pleased because I would spend time with my grandmother, Emma Vidal. She liked being called "Grandma Goose." After enjoying the festivities for a good minute, I finally asked, "When is Grandma Goose going to get here?"

My Aunt Monica took me to the side and explained that she had passed away two years earlier. Not being able to see her again was a bitter pill to swallow, but I had no one to blame but myself.

I kicked myself because I realized that my pride and anger got in the way of visiting her or any of the Vidals. And despite the time I reached out trying to bridge the distance after writing the *Honor Thy Father* article for Ebony Magazine and he "seemed" receptive, he fell back into his old ways of being a shadow. All the years of wanting my father to just "be there," and when it finally happened and I reconnected with him and he disappeared again, I just didn't care anymore. I didn't see the point, since I was already a grown man and could make the decision to move on since I had forgiven him for the past. His present actions stung a little because this time he couldn't lay the blame for his absence on anyone else, but I realized I did my part and maybe his silence was better for my path than anything else.

But in not caring about my father, I'd also given up on the members of the family who did care. My aunts, uncle, and cousins were always happy to see me when I came around. I had discounted the love of my grandmother and simply went on living life as if I had time. I now have an image of her in my living room where I can put eyes on that black and white photo of my grandmother in her younger years.

"Thank you, Grandma Goose, for the time that you were here," I whisper to her photo from time to time. "And thank you for our moments together."

That day I came back, my family reconnected me with her by recounting some of their memories and sharing priceless photos of her; the younger images before I was even thought of. Along with even more photos of the rest of the family. I learned who the Vidals really were and felt a missing part of myself fall into place.

Aunt Monica invited me over for Father's Day to be with my grandfather. I had been to his house a few times since, reconnecting with Aunt Monica and my cousins. He had divorced Grandma Goose and started a whole new life with a new wife while my father was still in grammar school.

Surprisingly, my Aunt Monica asked if my mother would come too. For the first time I could remember, my mother was nervous. She brought her own icebreaker, one of her infamous cocktails—the Naleighna Kai Special—to kick things off. She walked in, asked for directions to the kitchen and went straight to work making the Amaretto, white rum, pineapple, coconut, and raspberry sorbet frozen specialty. My aunts and cousins watched her put that magic together and soon everyone was at ease. They were tempting her with that good authentic Mexican food which she loved.

My grandfather watched it all from his seat at the head of the dining room table. He even demanded to have his own glass of that sweet concoction, even though he wasn't supposed to indulge.

Evidently, my Aunts Monica and Weda had not let my grandfather in on the game plan because the first thing he asked me was, "And how is your mother?"

An awkwardly hilarious silence ensued as my mother's head whipped toward the elderly man, and her eyebrows shot up.

I got over my shock and said, "Actually, grandfather, she's sitting right next to you."

My grandfather did a double take, and the embarrassment was all over his reddened face as he said, "Oh, I thought that was your girlfriend."

My mother roared with laughter as she replied, "You thought he was dragging the geriatric end of the dating pool?"

Everyone joined in her laughter as my grandfather shot back, "No I just thought he was into beautiful women."

Mom grinned and said, "Good comeback."

During the course of an outstanding meal and another round of those infamous drinks that had a few eyelids trying to make their way south, my grandfather gave a little history on Irondale, a place on the far southeast side of Chicago where everyone in the room had been raised, including my mother. The area also covered Jeffrey Manor and Trumbull Park. A great number of Blacks and Hispanics resided there.

"When I first came to America," my grandfather said, keeping his focus on me at the dinner table. "I found a job in the steel mills on the far east side of Chicago. I would get to work with my people, but I also planned to learn English. Unfortunately, no one spoke English while they were working. I knew if I wanted to make my way in America, I would need to be able to speak English well. I left that job and went looking for other work. I ended up at the tail end of Lake Shore Drive. That is the place where all of the boats and yachts are housed.

"There was a sign out that they were looking for a mechanic and that is the very thing that I did in Mexico. I was given the opportunity to work on the motor. They had taken something out of it, and in order to get the job, I had to figure out why it was not working. An easy fix, and they told me I would receive a call to let me know if I had the job.

"I did not make it even half a block before they brought me back and told me that I could start work that minute. I worked for them for over twenty years and learned English well. When the owners wished to retire, they wanted to sell the business to me. But I didn't have the kind of money to buy their business. I was a family man. Having a wife and raising children meant all my money went to them. So the owners did something unexpected. They loaned me the money to buy their business and let me pay them back in small installments.

So I went from being a man who came to America with the clothes on my back to a man who owned a building and business that covered a full city block. I had that business for years before I retired. I raised my family. I had one love of my life, then later another love of my life. And at some point, I will join her and be happy again. I love my family, my children, my grandchildren, and my great grandchildren, but I miss my wife."

"Grandpa, are you trying to check out of here?" I asked, concerned with the resigned and weary tone in the man's voice.

My grandfather looked directly at me and said, "When you find a woman that you love the way I love my wife, then you will understand."

Then he offered to let me take anything I wanted from the house and added, "But I am so glad you brought your beautiful mother with you." His eyebrows lifted in a comedic fashion. "Even if I thought she was the girlfriend."

Chicago Roots with Texas Boots

"You Have Chicago Roots with Texas Boots" is a saying by my tribe member, Yvonne Elliott. She's right about that.

My move to Houston was really a step out on faith. I had moved to Nashville, then back to Chicago after five years. I moved to South Carolina and ended up moving back home. Relocating to Texas wasn't the first time I shared a living space with an intimate partner. I was definitely hoping this was the last.

Most people would critique my decision as cavalier or stupid. I had only been to Houston for a tattoo convention with 9MAG Tattoo, and then to visit my girlfriend Donisha. Although we've known each other for a long time, (since Fisk), we hadn't even been in our relationship for a year at that time. I didn't know anyone else in Houston, didn't know much about the city. If the relationship failed, it would be a long way back to Chicago. Yet, I took the chance.

Being a freelance creative, I have one privilege that not

everyone has. I'm able to move around without having to worry about quitting a job. I'm able to work remotely from anywhere. If I wanted to be overseas right now, I could. It is a privilege I took for granted for years. Instead of embracing it, I was more worried about finding a stable job, when we all know that jobs are never stable.

When Donisha and I became exclusive, she let me know from the starting point that she had no plans on moving back to Chicago. So either I was moving to Houston or there was really no point in continuing the relationship. I honestly couldn't remember the last time someone was this direct with me in an intimate relationship. Most of my relationships have been, in my eyes, more going with the flow or just trying to figure out how to navigate. However, with Donisha, it was more like *This is what I expect if we are going to get into a relationship*, prompting further conversation about said expectations. I respected her because it didn't feel like she was giving an ultimatum, but more like an invitation, sort of like getting IKEA furniture, but with clearer assembly instructions.

If I wasn't up to it, we could've left it at that, and went on our merry way. I am no stranger to taking risks. When I walked across the stage to get that diploma from Columbia College, my decision to leave South Carolina has been a win-win for both sides and was worth the risk

However, I decided to take this one, a risk that has proven to be the best move for me. I packed my things and Donisha and I made the long drive to Houston.

Noah had long nights on the ark, where sunlight didn't touch him. He could only wonder if the darkness would ever end and life would begin again.

Life Interrupted

Life and Death

Mid October 2020, in the heart of the Covid-19 Pandemic, I started feeling a sting in the back of my throat. Houston weather had changed drastically from heat to freezing, and I wasn't prepared.

Donisha and I thought my discomfort was just something that would go away. Take some Vitamin C, some tea, and all would be well. But day after day, I gradually felt worse. I thought it was just a cold brought on by me not having a scarf or hat when I would go to the grocery store. I started taking cough drops. Then the fever hit, and other symptoms of the flu. It had to be the flu, and nothing more.

Donisha tried to keep me hopeful, but things became worse. I couldn't taste anything, and then my cough produced mucus that went from green to red. Over time, my fever didn't come down, and it became difficult to breathe. I would fall asleep and wake up gasping for air. I was also coughing up spots of blood. This definitely wasn't the flu. Donisha took me to get a Covid-19 test. The two to three days waiting for results seemed like forever. We received that email that said I tested positive. However, we were already informed there's not much that the hospitals could do. There wasn't a vaccine yet, and the only thing we could do was somewhat ease the pain with tea, Mucinex, and steam baths with vapor rub.

The first time we went to the hospital, I couldn't take it because my breathing became much worse. We were worried. I tried everything I could to get better, but this wasn't ordinary. The process was out of my hands. It's uncomfortable when you have to wait and see what happens, even when it doesn't look promising. Only certain hospitals were taking Covid-19 patients via the emergency room. Donisha found Ben Taub Hospital and drove me there. It was a scary moment for both of us because no visitors were allowed and I had to go in alone.

Even though we already knew that I tested positive, I needed help breathing and to get my fever down. I was willing to try anything they could do to make that better. However, after all the tests, poking, and blood draws, the only thing they were able to do for me was to let me know that I had pneumonia. Out of everything at their disposal, the only thing they could offer me was extra strength Tylenol. That didn't lift my spirits or calm my nerves. Post after post on Facebook and Instagram of friends whose family passed away due to Covid-19 was disheartening. So finding out that I had pneumonia was terrifying.

They sent me home.

I wish I could say I felt better over the next few days but that was not my reality. I started sleeping on the floor because that was the only cool place to lay my body. Donisha did everything in her power to make me feel comfortable, fixing me food even though I couldn't taste it, doing store runs for medications, all the above. I just wanted it to be over. I remember she told me I was talking in my sleep, having a conversation with no one physically present.

Later that night, Donisha shook me awake, saying, "We're going back to the hospital." Apparently, my breathing had stopped again during my sleep. I don't have a history of sleep apnea, so this was new to me. I kept hearing in my head what they said the last time I went. There's nothing else we can do.

Honestly, I didn't know if that would change.

She said:

My son had a few reservations about making that move to Houston because it meant that I would be in Chicago without a man around the house. At one point during a conversation he said, "Mom, my life would be complete if you were down here in Houston."

I let him know that I wouldn't ever want him to split his time between his Mama and his woman. When the grandbabies come, then I'll make that trip.

He became a "grill master," teasing us with photos of scrumptious meals. Shifting to a low-to-no carb diet led him to losing a nice amount of weight. I believe that had a positive impact when he was later hit with a health challenge that could have been much worse if he hadn't dropped those excess pounds.

While on a live Zoom event called, Love is an Inside Job, I

received a text from my son's beloved that said, "I'm rushing J. L. to the hospital." My entire world came to a standstill and I tried to regroup because I was in the middle of the event. I let the guests and panelist know about the text I received and all of the panelists immediately went into prayer. One by one ... Janice M. Allen (author of Growth), Janine A. Ingram (author of Born to Be Rich), Rev. Renee Sesvalah Cobb-Dishman (author of Speak it into Existence), Betty Clawson (author of If You Didn't Have it In You, You Wouldn't See it In Me), and Florenza Denise Lee (author of Purpose)—and more went into a tag team of amazing and powerful prayers for J.L's healing and for God to come in and do a miraculous work. I made it through the event, but I have to be honest with you ... I was not all right.

Because of travel restrictions at that time, I couldn't hop on a plane and be with him. And though I know the prayers were surrounding him, anxiety crept in from time to time. At one point, his life flashed before my eyes—all the beautiful parts of it. From childhood to the present day. I even pictured him in that hospital bed all alone and thought, "I hope they are doing the best by him and don't think he's worth more in parts."

Yes, it was that low for me thinking they would let him die so they could harvest his organs.

Don't Call it a Comeback

He said:

We followed the same routine as last time. Donisha had to wait in the car, and I had to go in alone. A lot of sick people were in the waiting area. Some looking how I felt and others looking even worse. Covid-19 was really kicking our butts. I had a new set of nurses and doctors this time. However, they all looked like they definitely needed some rest. Between hospitals being short-staffed and resources being scarce, they were doing the best they could.

I had my phone handy and kept Donisha and my cousin Erica in the loop since she works in the medical field. Donisha kept my mother informed as much as possible. The doctor ran a lot of tests, but mainly all efforts revolved around my breathing. She said they were going to admit me because my oxygen levels were not to her liking. All I could think was *thank God*, because we were tired of trying to figure this out on our own. If it were the flu, we could manage, but Donisha and I were way out of our league and there wasn't a shred of anything on Google besides WebMD. We knew to stay away from that site if we wanted to remain sane.

I've never had to stay in the hospital overnight before, so three-and-a-half days were torture. Not because of Ben Taub itself, but this wasn't any ordinary hospital stay. This was a quarantined stay, meaning no visits and I couldn't come out of the room. The first night was brutal. I couldn't sleep because anytime I started drifting off, the oxygen sensor would start beeping very loudly, indicating that my oxygen levels were too low. Even with the help of being put on oxygen, it only made a small difference. I managed to get sleep in five-minute increments, throughout the night. Certainly not enough to keep me fully functional or able to answer any questions the next day.

The nurses did the best they could to make my stay comfortable, but my body was going to have to just recover under God's will. The nurses and doctor coming to check on me was the only in-person human interaction I had during my stay. These visits lasted maybe fifteen minutes or less at a time. I was able to video chat and text Donisha, but it wasn't the same. I didn't know at the time how long I was going to be stuck in that room. I asked Donisha to bring my charger for my phone so that it wouldn't die on me and my book of Bahái Prayers. I definitely believe in God, however communication between us has been lackluster on my end. You hear all the time to pray even when things seem to be going right, but there's always that human element where I forget that I need God all the time and to remain grateful for everything He's done in my life.

Noah probably felt like all was lost when the water didn't recede. But a new beginning was coming, and it all rested on the shoulders of an unlikely ambassador—the dove.

The nurses were able to collect my things and bring them to me. Attached to the book was a letter from Donisha.

10/31/20
To the love of my Life,
I just wanted to remind you of how much I love you. You're going to get through this. I know it's scary, but you fight. We have memories to create, babies to make, and life to live. I'm praying for a speedy recovery.
Forever and Always Devoted to you,
Donisha

When things get complicated, you sometimes wonder if that person will stick. This may be the "realist" in me, but I don't think it's fair to expect someone to be there. Not everyone is built the same. It doesn't make them weak. They just know how much they are able to take. Even though this was not in our control, I know this was mentally and physically taxing on her. I sat there alone, crying, not because I was sad, but because I was grateful to have *My Person*. I was also grateful for the gesture. Something that anyone else could've decided to send through text, she took the time to write in a note so I would have something tangible. What some may see as a small thing, was a major thing to me.

That was a boost to my overall spirit. Between Donisha, my mother, Jon and Liezel, Aunt Monica, and my cousin Erica who constantly checked on me and advised me on everything that was going on from oxygen sensors to medication they were giving me, I felt a concentrated dose of love. I stayed off social media during that time because I didn't have the energy to post or explain what was going on. I also asked my mother, via a video chat, to not say anything on social media other than asking for prayers and positive energy. It wasn't just for my sake. I didn't want her to have to constantly explain what was happening to a whole bunch of people, no matter how close they were. That could be mentally taxing all together.

Then things took a turn for the worse.

She said:

Soon all the video chats texts ceased. My son couldn't talk or breathe. They were talking about putting him on a ventilator. The odds of him recovering were even slimmer. That's when I prayed for strength to handle whatever was in God's Will. Donisha was handling things like a champ and kept me updated on his progress or lack thereof. She held it together and I couldn't have done anything better if I were down there myself. I liked her before he moved to Texas. I loved her for her determination, tenacity, and strength when he needed it most.

When his breathing did not get better, faith took a nosedive, that's when I received a photo of him that one of the nurses had taken and it was a subliminal message that provided a sense of relief.

He said:

By the end of day three, I was losing it. I felt weak. Anytime I stood to go to the bathroom, I felt like I was going to black out. I also couldn't remember words, words that I would use on a normal basis. I just blanked out. Remembering certain things from my childhood became difficult and frustrating. I felt that if I stayed in that room, I was going to crack. I still couldn't get any sleep and the doctor still didn't like my oxygen levels even though they had improved. She instructed the nurse to give me a spirometer and said if I could get the ball to 4000 ml by the next day, I would be discharged. She left the room before I could even try to see where I stood. I could barely get it past 500 ml. I think she already knew, so she didn't even bother. I exercised my lungs with that thing every thirty minutes throughout the night. I already wasn't getting sleep so might as well try.

She came in around 11 in the morning to check my progress. I was able to reach 4000 ml. It hurt a little bit, but I made it.

She said, "You're really determined to get out of here, huh?"

I said, "Absolutely!" I was missing my own bed. I barely remembered what outside looked like. My only view was the other side of the building—just brick and windows. She agreed that I was able to be discharged but told me that I needed to keep up with the exercises. She also informed me that I tested negative, but I still needed to quarantine. I let Donisha know and she was on her way to pick me up. While I waited, I gave blood for antibodies, and did my discharge paperwork.

When I made it to the car, it felt surreal that I was there. Too tired and weak to cry, I was just grateful to have survived this far. There are countless others that were in that hospital. I don't know if they made it or not. The fact that many didn't stand a chance against that virus was a hard pill to swallow. I'm grateful to the doctors and nurses for their hard work. I'm grateful to my family and friends. Most of all, I'm grateful to God for placing Donisha in my life and keeping her safe. Through all the sickness and taking care of me, she risked her own health, but remained *My Person*, and I'm so grateful that through all of that, she tested negative.

* * *

Talking with my amazing supervisor a few months later, I opened up about my COVID-19 experience and although I've mostly recovered from it physically, I had to acknowledge that mentally I haven't. You think that just because you're able to breathe on your own and walk around that it doesn't give you a different outlook on life. While some had gone into the "seize the moment" mentality, my mind went into guilt and quite a bit of fear.

I am grateful to be here and to be alive. I'm grateful for my health, and my fiancée's health, and for her being with me through all of that. But I can't say that I don't think about the countless others who have made their transition during the outbreak. I can't say that I wasn't confronted with my own mortality and questioning how soon or far away that day is for me. The experience kind of made me not want to go anywhere or do anything because I'm constantly thinking about how fragile life is. Honestly, writing is the first time I feel I've been able to put it into real words.

Several months after the experience, I feel like I took a small step back into being myself again. Versus taking an Uber home from the doctor, halfway home I actually caught the bus for the first time, then walked the rest of the way. I listened to Lebron James on the Calm App and just enjoyed seeing the neighborhood. It even rained on my head halfway through and I was okay with it—it's just water. So weird how much good a simple walk can do.

I am so thankful to all of those who prayed for me and interceded on my behalf when I couldn't say a word. Donisha and my mother were at the forefront, and everyone played a part in sending God the message for my health and healing. I held onto my prayer book, but everyone who put up those prayers had a direct line to God!

Thank you.

Thinking of a Master Plan

Husband. Family man. Provider. Friend. All the things that a man should be to the woman he loves, but not nearly the example that I had grown up with.

On our first year anniversary in 2020, way before I tested positive for COVID-19, Donisha and I ended up celebrating in the house. Not the most ideal scenario, but we made do with everything going on. We ate dinner, which I picked up from The Cheesecake Factory. After that, I suggested that we write letters to each other, seal them in an envelope, and crack them open to read to each other on our next anniversary. I figured it could be a meaningful way to share our love because writing letters is such a rare thing nowadays. However, my letter to Donisha, was my actual proposal.

I had been thinking about it for some time. Even though we hadn't been in a relationship that long, I knew she was the one I wanted to marry. Everything seemed to fall into place. I loved her, my mother loved her, I loved her mother and sister. But the major thing I paid attention to was her interaction with me. My previous relationships served their purpose, with some positive moments and some negative ones, but lots of lessons learned. However, Donisha's communication is beyond top tier. She knows how to have a conversation. Even if it's a tough one, we're able to deal with our feelings in an adult way. No shouting matches, name calling, furniture flying, and no saying anything that we can't take back. We don't always agree but it doesn't ever get disrespectful. She is also a person who knows what she wants, except when it comes to food. But I feel like I found my life partner and someone I can call my best friend.

Even before we hit our anniversary, I asked her previous roommate, Drea, to get her ring size. So, early on this was already set in motion. I think that's what made it great, but also frustrating due to the anticipation. Sitting on something this major for a whole year was torture, especially when you want to hurry up and get it on. Battling between, "Anytime is the right time," and "Nope, just wait and fully plan it out," was a roller coaster.

Then there was the other problem: I'm not that big of a planner. On my first try at planning the proposal, I had the bright idea to propose on the Yard at Fisk University where we first met. I wanted all of our friends and family to be there. I stuck with that plan for a while, forgetting one major thing: we're in a pandemic with no vaccine. I couldn't take a chance.

I brought reinforcements. I first told my mother that I was going to propose, but I just wanted her to be there with me. I then contacted Donisha's sister, Katala, her best friends, Ive, Megan, and Lauren. I was trying to figure out where we were going to be able to pull it off. I still wanted our friends and family there but didn't want anyone to be exposed. I believe it was Katala or Megan who recommended Buckingham Fountain, a great and open place with amazing Chicago skyline views. Knowing that Chicago weather always fluctuates, especially in spring, I was worried about the rain. The backup location would have to be somewhere nearby—Navy Pier. Over time, we all put our heads together to make sure it was special, and as Donisha's sister and friends would say, "Just as extra as she is."

Then another wrench was thrown in the plans. Donisha wanted to go to Tulum for our anniversary. She was very insistent on being somewhere warm. I came up with the "story" that I was needed in Chicago that weekend, because my mother was being honored for her literary contributions and it was the day before our anniversary. So we would have to be in Chicago and could possibly head out the day after. Time went on, and I decided not to mention anything about Tulum to make sure things would shift to Chicago and my plan. Donisha came to the conclusion that we wouldn't be able to travel to Tulum because we hadn't secured any tickets or reservations. Bullet dodged.

Another plan that I had was to ask her mother and sister in person for her hand in marriage when I was supposed to come home in April. The event was cancelled, so I didn't have a good excuse to go home. Instead, I asked them via phone because I still wanted to make that part happen.

The team and I went back and forth about switching the location, because Katala informed me that Buckingham Fountain wouldn't be up and running until the weekend after. We were concerned the proposal wouldn't have the same luster if the fountain wasn't on. We decided to stick with the plan and have Navy Pier as a backup. Buckingham Fountain was more conveniently located, with open space and plenty of fresh air. Navy Pier was like a mall, so even with mask mandates lifting, I didn't want to run the risk of being in a place that was too crowded.

Even though it seemed like there was roadblock after roadblock, my main concern was making everything go as planned in Chicago. I went a day ahead because I still had to stick with my mother's "Literary Award" story, but it was also to check into our hotel and pick up the rental car. Normally I would drive my mother's SUV, but she was bringing people to the proposal. And of course, it rained that day.

Things were not looking good for the home team.

The day of the proposal, it rained earlier in the morning and I was just praying the sun would come out. Dark clouds passed by throughout the day. Ive and Lauren picked her up from the airport and drove her around while I finished the final touches. When she made it to the hotel, she wore this shirt made by her cousin Dee that said, "I Love Jeremy." We went down the Mag Mile so she could grab a few things that she forgot to pack. The sun came out and I stopped for a moment, took my phone out, switched it to the camera, pointed at the sky and said, "Stay," while snapping a photo. Donisha looked at me with this confused, yet hilarious look.

She said:

Positivity can move mountains, but the real question is do we let it move that mountain or do we allow doubt to come in and that mountain to stay in place?

My son coordinated a surprise proposal for his girlfriend. They live in Houston, but both of them are from Chicago. He worked with her family and friends to pull it off. He held to that thought of the proposal taking place in Chicago in front of Buckingham Fountain. It was their dating anniversary and she wanted to go out of the country. So that was a mountain, but with all of the restrictions in place during these more interesting times, she decided against it. He could breathe and everything was on point for a Chicago proposal.

The weather leading up to the date had been wavering between calm and storms, and it was supposed to rain that day.

"Son," I said checking the weather on the phone. "You might need to make other arrangements."

"It's not going to rain on my proposal, Mom."

"Maybe you should move it to Navy Pier."

He replied, "It's not going to rain on my proposal, Mom."

I disconnected the call, and the sky became much darker. I called him back and said, "Maybe we should move it to the restaurant."

"It's not going to rain on my proposal, Mom."

The closer it came to time for me to leave to go downtown to Buckingham Fountain, the more my heart pounded in my chest because the sky was still overcast. The sun wasn't even thinking about coming out. Only later would I find out that there had been a little doubt in his mind early on, but he swept it aside and held to the vision of the sun shining on them.

When I made it to the car and put my hand on the steering wheel, the first sign of the sun came out. It peered from behind a cloud and I texted him that I was on my way. He wrote back, *We will see you there.*

Please Don't Kill My Vibe

He said:

We returned to the hotel and dressed for our anniversary dinner. I had brought my suit that didn't seem to fit anymore. We had just finished an egg fast the week prior, so the suit was much too big.

I made reservations at Tango Sur, an Argentinian steakhouse. I wasn't sure how she was feeling about the date since it was technically a little early. People were just getting off work and we were in our Sunday best.

In the weeks prior to the proposal, I was afraid she was catching on because she said that family and friends were acting weird. I had an idea that would hopefully throw her off. The team thought the plan was funny, but we were also worried she was going to strangle me at the dinner table. During dinner, I pulled out a black case from my pocket, opened it and handed it to her.

I braced myself. But she looked at those earrings in a ring box and said they were so beautiful. Thank God, this wasn't one of those moments from the movies where the woman would have splashed water in the man's face for tricking her like that. She did manage to say jokingly, "They are so pretty, but also don't be pulling a box like this from under the table. You know you petty for that right?" We both just laughed.

After dinner, I snapped a few photos of her in a beautiful black and white dress, standing by some plants. When we got in the car, I put the GPS in but Siri kind of spoiled it by yelling out the destination. Donisha started asking, "What's next?" To throw her off again, I told her a photographer was meeting us at Buckingham Fountain for a photoshoot. When we arrived, I forgot how long of a walk it was, even with parking across the street. So I let her keep her flats on until we came close to the intended destination.

When we made it to the fountain, I told her the photographer was on the other side. I helped her slide into her heels and we started walking slowly around the fountain.

She looked toward her right and said, "There's a lot of people over there. Looks like a celebration." We noticed all the balloons and matching colors.

I said, "Yeah, they might be there for a balloon release or something."

We just kept walking, and then she asked, "Is that my sister?"

I played dumb and said, "Huh?"

She asked again, "Is that my sister?"

Still playing dumb, and also because she has better eyesight than I do, I asked, "Where?"

Donisha replied, "Right there with the white shorts," and pointed towards the group.

I just shrugged.

We came closer, then she asked and her voice raised an octave with each question, "Is that your momma? Is that *my* Momma? Kevin?"

My mother, Katala, and Donisha's mother approached us with purple rose petals lining the ground. We all hugged, and the crowd of people walked towards us.

Donisha chuckled asking, "Why is my entire life here?" Our family and friends where there, physically, spiritually, and virtually, with Kevin holding my mother's iPad for the Zoom that was being live streamed to a private FB Group.

This is when my legs began to shake. I was slightly nervous before, but in that moment my nerves were shot. This is a big step. It's not just asking the important question, it's also the responsibility that comes with it. Being able to take care of and provide for that person. Them trusting you with their protection and security, and being there for the hard times, just as you would be there for the good ones. I've only witnessed this a few times in my life, so I didn't have many examples to draw from. But that didn't mean I couldn't take on the responsibility. That meant that before I asked the question, I knew what I wanted to do. I knew how I wanted my marriage to work and how we worked together. We have each other and we have a great support system.

What I had planned to say went totally out of my mind. I was just happy in that moment. I looked around at everyone who was there, and the team of people who were integral in making this happen. I was beyond grateful. But the question still needed to be asked. While getting down on one knee, I thought about the fact that I wish I could've done this for us when we were younger. Not because so much time had passed, but because I knew I was going to need a little help getting up. I liked her back in 2005, but that wasn't our time. I'm grateful for our now because I felt we were made to be together.

My grandfather had said, "When you find a woman that you love the way I love my wife, then you will understand."

I took out an envelope from my inside pocket. It contained the letters we had written to each other on our prior anniversary and sealed away to be read on this day a year later. I was going to open it and read, but I was already having a hard time speaking. So, I opted to just speak from my heart.

"You have changed my life so much. You have done so much for me. I cannot imagine life without you and I want to spend the rest of my life with you, but you already knew that. Would you do me the honor of being my wife?"

Tears were falling from her eyes as she nodded yes and said, "You are things I didn't think to ask God for."

What a statement. What a woman!

She said

Let me tell y'all, the sun came all the way out, dried up everything and kept shining for the rest of the day. I should have believed him because sometimes his faith is stronger than mine. When he was in the hospital and they had him hooked up to tubes, he had the nurses send me a picture of him with his prayer book and his phone charger in his hand. He couldn't talk. He could barely breathe, but he wanted me to see that image to let me know that either way, he was going to be all right.

Now I'm going to be honest, if he tries that weather thing for the wedding, I'm going to pass out. But on the day of his engagement, he climbed that mountain, went around it, and right through it.

A few weeks later, I was in a room on Clubhouse and the international bestselling author of the *50 Shades of Grey* series was on the stage. I told the story surrounding my son's amazing proposal. Erika L. James opened her mic along with everyone else and said she was in tears.

Then a guy at the bottom of the photo interrupted by opening his mic and started laying on the compliments and praise to Erika and the room went totally silent for like thirty seconds. He said something else directly to her, putting her on the spot so she was forced to respond. Once, and there was total silence from everyone again, probably because they couldn't believe he'd done such a thing. Finally, the moderator said, "This is pretty awkward and I'm sure it's making Erika uncomfortable." Erika opened her mic again and said, "Can we get back to the proposal? I want to hear more of that. I'm still crying."

Everyone in the room opened up and went in, agreeing. People love a good romance.

Don't Have Me Crying in Costco

She said:

Now here's where I know that I'm on the path to manifesting healthier relationships. Earlier, we wrote about when my son was home from college and I thought he needed a little shaking up in order to get him on a more productive path. Part of the issue was a lesson in *sweat equity*—when you're not giving as much to a household financially, you can give it by doing more around the house.

He was not feeling that. And I wasn't feeling the fact that he wasn't feeling that.

My action—putting him out of the house—was totally correct. The timing of it was all wrong. And it was the first time we ever had a break in our relationship.

One day, I opened a video chat and found that he was in Costco. I told him to call me back when he had a moment. He said he could talk right then. I apologized to him for what had happened years earlier.

He said, "Come on, Mom, don't have me crying in Costco." Then, as he held back tears he said, "I forgave you a long time ago."

This is the second time I have felt deeply compelled to explore my actions.

A week after that, I received a video call from him. This time, he wanted to apologize to me. Evidently, he had come to an understanding of his own, realizing what I meant all those years ago. *He* apologized to *me*. And I said while in the comfort of my home, "Come on son, don't have me crying in Costco."

We both laughed.

Then   Now

Ain't No Half-Stepping

Things are looking up.

When I'm told to just focus on one of my gifts, I really bristle at hearing those words. Why can't I be a master at multiple things?

In 2018, I purchased my first professional camera and was literally thrust into photography and videography mainly because people saw that I had talent. Same way that it happened with my writing career, where those seven pages ushered in a whole new chapter in my life. Others saw that vision before I did. I still had to put in that work, though. However, I was more concerned with the fact that I was still learning how to use the camera while actually doing the job.

Like Noah, I had to follow God's instruction because it led me to the next part of my path. Even when I didn't know exactly where it would lead. God didn't say it would be easy. Didn't say that Noah wouldn't feel some pain or have doubts along the way. God simply gave him the tools to make the successful transition from one aspect of his life to the next.

Fast Forward—I took a series of photos on the rooftop back in October 2019 in Chicago. The weather was frigid and unforgiving during that long climb up an abandoned stairwell. I didn't do anything with the images I took that day because honestly, I hated that the clouds didn't provide enough sunshine and doubted anything could be done with them. Lately, I've been revisiting some photos that I've taken and decided to take a stab at it again, only to realize, I've literally been sitting on a gold mine and didn't recognize it because I doubted my gift.

So, pushing beyond my doubts and fears, I did a deep dive into the things I love to do, which meant embracing my creative side. Photography. Videography. Graphic Design. Brand Management. At first, I was taking on clients because I was happy that people wanted me to work on their projects. Then I learned a valuable lesson after a message from someone I consider a good friend and mentor in design. Her words really hit home. I needed to set real boundaries in my personal life and in business. Chris Do, another mentor, has said the same thing. Another thing I learned from him is to charge what you're worth. You don't want to resent the client or the work.

During the conversation with my friend, I listed all of the things I have to do during the week and sometimes weekends, especially with recent transitions. I'm designing, sketching, culling through photos, reading, project planning, learning UX Design, staying up-to-date on Art & Design, starting back my livestream, podcasting, and I still have to work for my 9-until. Oh yeah—and I have a life, too—*wedding planning*, and so much more. (On that note, if I never have another taste of wedding cake for the rest of my life, I'm all the way good!)

I have burnt out plenty of times before and it definitely took a toll on me. My life and path is growing and it's only going to get bigger. That's the plan at least. I'm only one person. I had to set a few boundaries:

The result of making this adjustment, embracing self-care, and protecting my mental health means I don't work for anyone or anything on the weekends. That time is dedicated to getting my life/energy together, enjoying my time with my beloved, connecting with family and friends in a non-business-related way, and enjoying the things that I want to do.

Time is something that shouldn't be wasted, especially with all that I have going on. I'm in the process of working with other creatives. I hired a virtual personal assistant to keep up with work and my calendar. Delegation is a good thing.

These are just some of the ways I'm changing up things for the better. I appreciate my clients, family, and friends. However, I now realize I also have to take care of myself. My mother says she wished she had learned this lesson early in her life.

See, there are some things she's learning from me. And that includes the fact that I'm sometimes the parent in our relationship.

"Mom, your bedtime is 11:00 p.m." This is something I had to put in place because she was all out in those Clubhouse streets hopping from room to room. I received a notification every time and couldn't believe she was living off three hours of sleep.

"Mom, I see an awful lot of take-out coming into the house and no groceries." This came after watching her on the home camera. Once, she thought she was slick and didn't drop me a text to let me know she was pulling up. She tipped into the house with a big container of sweet tea, knowing good and well she didn't need any of that. So, I sent her a text after I rolled the footage back to see what she was up to and typed, "Lay off that sweet tea! I saw that McDonald's walking in with you." Busted!

Not to mention getting her to wear a hat when it's so cold she can see her breath in front of her. She finally gave in and bought one.

The biggest lesson I imparted to my mother was the difference between "listening" and "hearing." My mother is the multi-task queen, but what I found was that she would not be "present" for conversations at times. So once I said, "Mom, I'm going to let you go so you can focus on what you're doing." She looked up at the camera and said, "But I'm talking to you." I replied, "Yes, you're listening, but you're not hearing me. I can tell when you've zoned out of the conversation even though you can repeat every word back to me."

From that point on, whenever I call, or anyone else calls, she tries to give her undivided attention. Who knew that one day I would be imparting wisdom to the woman whose wisdom had guided me from birth and beyond?

Life is a funny thing. Just when you think you have it all figured out, there's another bend in the road. You learn to lean in when the winds start howling and the challenges are snapping at your feet. I think of Noah and his impossible mission made possible. I think of his Spiritual Father guiding his every step and picking him up when he fell.

I think of the woman that carried me in her womb against impossible odds and how she was there holding my hand as I learned to walk. From the sidelines, she cheered me on imparting ribbons of love and wisdom with every word she spoke and wrote. And when I fell, as we often do, I see her still there on the sidelines willing me to stand; willing me to trust in my own abilities. I think of Noah and my Tribes—the one from my childhood and the several that surround me now. I think of the new beginning with my soulmate at my side, and all that the future holds. I look down at my feet on a new path and I laugh out loud. There's no more rain in the cloud and no snow on the ground.

Only a dove bringing me an olive leaf as a sign of hope.

Afterword

In loving memory . . .

On April 3, 2020, I along with my OHMC (Olive-Harvey Middle College High School). and TCS (Triumphant Charter School) Family were hit hard. Helen Hawkins, our principal, chief, mentor, other mother, all of the above, made her transition.

This is the amazing woman who transformed all of us at Olive-Harvey Middle College High School. If it wasn't for her, I would've never graduated high school on time. I would have never gone on an HBCU College Tour. I would have never attended Fisk University on a full scholarship. Without her, I would've never had a Mr. Reynolds (R.I.P.) in my life as an English Teacher. I would've never had an Arthur Cuda G. McClellon (R.I.P.) to coach and mentor a lot of amazing men at my high school. We owe a debt that we cannot repay to these wonderful souls. They believed in us. They guided us. We are better because of them.

Mr. Reynolds was the first teacher I connected with at OHMC. He was my English Teacher, and not any ordinary teacher. He made English class fun and engaging. He was also the most relatable teacher because he was never too proud to share his story about how OHMC and Mrs. Hawkins helped him get to where he is, just like he was doing for us. He always correlated any English lesson back to African American history and the writings of the Harlem Renaissance.

People talk about representation now, but I was fortunate enough to have Mr. Reynolds to make sure I saw myself in every piece of Black history. From the leaders and artists that aren't often talked about, to the man who shares my last name and founded Black History Month—Carter G. Woodson. If it weren't for Mr. Reynolds, I honestly believe I would've gone through life without knowing a Black (Haitian) man by the name of Jean Baptiste Pointe DuSable was the founder of Chicago, the place where I was born. I wouldn't know about the walk of fame in Bronzeville. I wouldn't know Negro Spirituals were more than just *Wade in the Water*. Mr. Reynolds was more than just an English teacher. He was a griot who was able to do all of that while wearing the coolest outfits.

Rest in Peace Mr. Jones (AKA Falcon Punch). Definitely another harsh blow to the OHMC family. He was *the* smoothest, most profound teacher, teaching our Manhood Class in High School.

* * *

Most of my life, I've been surrounded by powerful and loving women. However, my mother made sure I had a pretty decent balance of male role models with positive influences. They weren't just anyone, they were men who could teach me things that my mother couldn't. Shihan Paul "Deno" Thomas, was one of those men. I was introduced to him, when I was at Tankson's Martial Arts. He was a big burley guy, and I originally thought he was mean. Not because he did anything to me, but reminded me of Ice Cube's face, just naturally fierce. I remember, he had a way of telling stories or sharing knowledge and it was always with a cigar or a pipe in his hand.

I transferred over to his karate school, Deno's Martial Arts and it was like being thrust to the forefront. Tankson's was a very good program, however having a good program means a lot of kids were lining up to get in. Deno's was a very personal setting as he started the karate school in 1995, but it was a more intimate setting and the best thing for me. Shihan Deno, worked with me and molded me into a young man by pushing me to be the best version of myself. I learned discipline and responsibility and if I got out of line, I would hate to be in class. Looking back on it, it wasn't as bad as getting a whooping. He taught me the art of winning, sometimes you win and sometimes you lose, but there's a chance to get it right again.

He wasn't a man that would just tell you how to be a man. He taught by example and put you in situations that would test you and your character. I was only a blue belt when he had me teaching the class. One time, it wasn't because he wanted me to, he actually fell asleep in the gym chair before class started. He was in a deep sleep, and I was almost afraid he was dead. His snore was a pretty loud indicator he was still with us. I ended up teaching the class and by the time he woke up, we were finished and bowing out. It felt great to teach, but also to just have the knowledge that I could get my classmates through a session.

I toured with him, winning tournament after tournament. I

even placed 1st nationally in my division for sparring and kata in the American Karate Association. I learned a lot during that time and I grateful for what Shihan Deno has done. Some people get into Karate because they want to fight or they've seen Bruce Lee or Jackie Chan in films or even want to do a bicycle kick like Liu Kang from Mortal Kombat. But I was there to learn how to defend myself if a fight ever occurred and to never go looking for one. I was there to train my mind to be strong, to analyze a situation and proceed accordingly. I was there to witness how a great man acts.

Shihan Deno passed when I was a freshman in college. I hate the fact that I didn't get a chance to see him one last time. But every now and then there's something that reminds me of him. It could be a story that I have during that time or just the smell of a cherry cigar. I'm just grateful that my mother brought Shihan Deno in my life.

***

Four weeks from finalizing this book, I woke up from some good sleep with a good dream. My 8th grade teacher/principal visited me in this dream. We were talking and she was asking me how I was doing. I haven't seen Ms. Whited since maybe 2005. So, it was like I was catching up with her in this dream. It was awesome talking to her. When I woke up, I Googled her, because I knew she was retired and teaching Aikido. The first thing I'm met with on the search was "Wendy Whited Obituary". Sure enough, she passed away in the past September.

Just a few words about her from my perspective. She was a bada$$, super awesome human being. She was one of the very few reasons I enjoyed going to Burnham School. I don't have many good memories being there, but Ms. Whited was what got me on the bus to school. She would talk to me about karate (especially when she found out I was practicing) and other things.

When I made it to her 8th grade class, that's when I had the most fights in school. I didn't go looking for them, but I got tired of avoiding them and being told by my teachers to just walk away by my teachers. Even though my mother said, "If someone touches you, you whoop that ass". I think Ms. Whited was the only one who understood. Once I was suspended for three days and she said I needed to take those days because I needed to regain some self-control, whether I'm defending myself or not. I liked Ms. Whited because she was real as a person and a real teacher, not just in school subjects, but life outside those four walls.

R.I.P. Ms. Whited. Thanks for coming to visit me.

More photo memories

Olive Harvey Middle College Memories

Hanging with my high school and college friends

That night at the Cavalcade of Authors and I said I wasn't up for speaking. Then Mom let loose with an embarrassing story and I made a miraculous recovery and took over.

About J. L. Woodson

J.L. Woodson, a native Chicagoan, began his career in the literary industry at sixteen years old as the award-winning author of The Things I Could Tell You, Super Woman's Child: Son of a Single Mother which was Nominated for an NAACP Image Award), as well as a short story in the NAACP Image Award-Winning Anthology, Breaking The Cycle presented by a New York Times Bestselling author.

His career area shifted to Graphic Design in 2009, creating Book Covers, websites, and other marketing materials for New York Times and National bestselling authors as well as independently published authors. During that year he also founded, Woodson Creative Studio, and has dedicated his company to providing high-quality Book Cover Design as well as other Graphic and Web Design support for his clients.

J.L. believes that every great story should have a wonderfully designed book cover wrapped around it, one that will capture the eyes and interest of a potential reader. Some of his clients include New York Times Bestselling authors Brenda Jackson and Mary B. Morrison, USA Today Best-selling authors Naleighna Kai, and National Bestselling authors, Martha Kennerson, Shakir

Rashaan, Susan D. Peters, J. L. Campbell, Karen D. Bradley, Lisa Dodson, Stephanie M. Freeman and many authors.

He is a Graduate of Columbia College Chicago, with a Degree in Graphic Design. He is an active member of AIGA (The American Institute of Graphic Arts), The One Club, and CAA (College Art Association). He splits his time working on design projects for businesses, corporations as well as traveling for different Design and Literary Events.

The Things I Could Tell You
[This is the book that launched J. L. Woodson's literary career at fifteen years old. These are the pages from the English Assignment]

Prologue

Cameron Spears thought his nightmares were over. September 17th would prove him both dead wrong and right—at the same time.

The cold air woke him suddenly. Something was wrong. It shouldn't be this cold in his bedroom. Seeing how his mom liked it hot and the Memphis sun could go from sizzle to crispy in record time, it often felt 180 degrees in the house.

He rolled over and glanced at the clock next to his bed, barely a minute after seven o'clock—dark outside and even darker in the room. Cameron's girlfriend, Larissa, was still asleep on the other end of his bed with her slender arms wrapped around his blue pillow, in the same peaceful way as when they went to Napville.

His mom would kill him if she walked in—even though they were on opposite ends of the bed and hadn't done anything. His mom trusted him. She said it was his hormones she didn't trust.

He glanced over at the slender girl sleeping as if she didn't have a care in the world. Larissa's dark brown hair flowed freely through his fingers, her coffee-colored skin glowing from the faint light coming from the street lamp in front of his house. Everything seemed normal, but something still wasn't right.

His eyes narrowed. Wait a minute! Dark in his room? The light wasn't on anymore. He didn't remember turning it off. He was sure he hadn't. Maybe Mom had done it? He swallowed hard, scanning the room. The navy blue curtains lifted and flowed into the room like cascading water allowing a little light to come in. The window was open. It was closed when he went to sleep. Something definitely wasn't right.

Instantly alert, he stood slowly, trying not to disturb Larissa. A small slice of fear stabbed his heart. His gaze flashed to Larissa. Still sleeping. He scanned the room again. A loud creaking noise by his closet door startled him. His blood turned to ice as a voice carried across the bedroom. "Hello, Cameron."

Cameron's heart skipped a beat, then his breathing slowed.

He turned around. A man crouched in the shadowed corner of his room. Cameron couldn't see the face until seconds later when the figure walked toward him. The faint light from outside fell just above his face. The shadow stepped closer to where the moonlight sliced his room in half. Cameron shuddered. The man held a gun. He also saw a familiar face covered with a thick beard, longer hair, and wrinkles that weren't there before. The man's plaid shirt and blue jeans were just as wrinkled as his face.

Looking in the man's blazing, brown eyes, Cameron shivered.

Those eyes gave him away. They were the same ones that looked up at Cameron from the living room floor in Chicago three years ago, where his father lay with a bullet in his chest and blood pouring out onto the white carpet. His mom stood holding a smoking gun. The nights of screaming, shouting, and beatings were finally over. His mother served no time for the shooting. Self-defense. His father, however, recovered and received a sentence for attempted murder.

The gun now pointing toward Cameron's chest was a nightmare come true. How did Ramon Rodriguez find them? After his father made several threats on his mom's life, she changed their last name, took Cameron and his little sister Andrea, and moved to Memphis, Tennessee hoping his father would never find them. Cameron would soon learn that nothing ever worked as planned. There were some things Cameron could tell anyone who would listen, because even young people's memories kept deadly secrets adults could only imagine.

They told no one where they were going, not even family. Then one day last week they received a letter from his mom's lawyer stating that Ramon had been released from prison a few days before. All week Cameron couldn't shake the feeling that his father was coming after them. For three years they had been safe and happy while neatly tucked away in the quiet suburban area of Shelby County. They had hoped to leave the past and violence behind them in Chicago.

Images from Chicago filled Cameron's head with fear. Looking at the silver gun pointed at his chest, Cameron realized—sometimes trouble was destined to follow, regardless of the location or how happy they were now.

A creak from the bed made his head snap around. Larissa's eyes bulged as if she were about to scream. His father's gun instantly focused on her.

As Cameron sprinted to Larissa, the clicking of the hammer as it cocked back on the gun meant his father was ready to pull the trigger, "Hey, no sudden moves." His father's voice was slurred. Not a good sign.

Cameron covered Larissa's mouth with his trembling hand. He whispered, "Listen to me, if you scream he'll kill us. We'll work this out somehow. Stick with me on this, okay?"

Terrified, Larissa nodded and reached for his hand, pulling it into hers. He hoped his strength would give her hope.

Cameron was about to sit next to her when his father's coldhearted voice instructed, "Stand up!"

"Yes sir." Addressing his father, or any adult that way, was a part of his nature. But any respect he had for his father died a decade ago.

"Call Anna."

"Yes . . . Sir," Cameron said, trying to keep the fear from his voice as he moved toward the door to call his mom. How could he warn his mom before she came upstairs?

"Stop," his father snapped as Cameron reached the threshold, "call her from there."

Cameron hesitated before yelling, "Mom!!!" His voice carried swiftly through the split-level ranch house.

After a while she called, "What is it, Cameron?"

"Can you come up here, please? I need your help."

"Sure, just give me a minute. Let me turn the fire down."

Did she hear the fear in his voice? Didn't she feel the chill in the air? Why hadn't he called her by her first name? That would have let her know that something was wrong.

"Back inside, Son," stopped any possibility of getting to his mom first.

Minutes seemed like hours as rain, beginning to pour down heavily, made loud thumping noises on the roof. Cameron watched his father. The man was shaking and sweating as though the room were a sauna. His father was high again. Cameron should have known.

Soft footsteps sounded like heartbeats on the stairs. His father stepped back halfway into the dark corner with the gun pointed at the doorway, waiting. The cold, gruff voice said, "Sit on the bed next to the girl."

His mom strolled in drying her hands on an apron. Cameron tried to signal her with expressions and quick hand movements. She didn't notice a thing.

"Hey." She said, flipping on the switch. "I told you about keeping the lights—"

A roaring thunder filled the whole room. The bitter smell of gunpowder flowed through the air like mist on a dreary Chicago night.

Blood splattered on the floor as his mom cried out. Seeing the bullet hole in her thigh, all Cameron could do was pray that his little sister wouldn't come in to find out what was going on. His father glanced at the trembling woman on the floor. Her thick hair framed her face. Her dark brown face twisted in pain. The blood flowed out onto her baby blue pants like a leaky faucet spewing water onto a kitchen floor.

Larissa snatched Cameron's Algebra book off the floor and threw it at his father. The book missed. Not that it would matter since it was the lightest book Cameron brought home from school.

Ramon pointed the gun at Larissa. Her almond shaped eyes

widened. As Ramon turned to Cameron, he smiled slyly, lowering the gun to his side. "Watch your girl. Make sure she doesn't do anything else stupid."

Losing interest in Larissa, Ramon turned his attention back to Cameron's mom lying helpless on the floor. Cameron rushed at his father, then stopped cold as the gun whirled in his direction. His father's reflexes weren't hampered by the drugs. Cameron could do nothing without his father noticing, so he approached Larissa and held her tight in his arms. His father immediately turned to the bleeding figure on the floor. "I waited a long time for this. Now you know what it feels like—," he growled, standing over her.

As Ramon called his mother a dirty name, the blood boiled in Cameron's veins. He wasn't going to let *anyone* talk to his mom like that. Especially if he is the man who caused so much trouble. More angry than afraid as his father kept talking, Cameron stopped listening and opened his mouth to speak. Something moved toward the doorway. He signaled his thirteen-year-old sister, Andrea, to stay back as his father's attention focused totally on his mom.

For once Andrea paid attention. Her thick ponytail whipped around as the rest of her body jerked to a halt. Cameron signaled with his hand about the gun, then put his thumb to his ear and his pinky toward his lips, mouthing the words "Call the police." Andrea nodded and inched back, a faint flash of disobedience gleaming in her eyes.

Cameron's father continued to verbally abuse his mother. Cameron held his breath, praying with all his heart.

Moments later Andrea did something none of them ever expected. She stood in the doorway, struggling with a gun. His mom kept it in the shoe box on the bottom of her bedroom closet. Cameron thought he was the only one who knew about it. He had repeatedly asked his mom to get rid of it. Keeping it there was like asking for his father to come after them., something similar to a jinx. Why didn't she listen to him? Why did seeing Andrea holding it make him feel better?

Startled, Ramon aimed his gun at the timid Andrea, eyes flashing with annoyance. Then he smiled and lowered his gun. "Hey, Sunshine. Give that to daddy."

Cameron jumped off the bed, intending to push Andrea out of the way. Instead he landed on the floor face first. He tried to stand, but remained tangled in the covers. Who knew that fear could make a person so clumsy?

A flash of light. Another roar of thunder.

Cameron's head snapped up. Andrea was still standing. No blood came from her body, but all color drained from her light golden skin. Cameron sighed with relief watching his father's bloodshot eyes widen as he dropped the gun on the floor. Holding his stomach, he fell to his knees with a solid thud, then to the hardwood floor landing on top of his gun. Using his foot, Cameron turned his body on his back. The rise and fall of his chest meant Ramon was down, but not dead. Larissa rapidly jumped out of the bed, grabbed the cordless phone off the nightstand, and dialed as she went to help his mom.

Cameron looked over at his sister once again. Smoke flowed from the gun as she let it fall by her side and cried. Their father had been her idol, and could do no wrong in her eyes. He had always spoiled her. She never knew their parents' fights weren't normal. Andrea had never understood.

"Here, I'll take this," Cameron said, slowly removing the gun from her stiff fingers. She stared blindly ahead. She didn't kill him, but shooting him took recognizing, for the first time, that their father could, and would hurt them. Tears continued to fall from her eyes. She kneeled next to their mom, took the pink bandana off her head, applying a little pressure to the wounded thigh.

Cameron inhaled deeply. His father had tortured his family enough. The law didn't protect them. Prison couldn't hold him. But Cameron could make it so that Ramon Rodriquez never bothered them again. Cameron pointed the gun at his head and cocked the hammer back. Strangely enough, his father had taught him and Andrea how to use a gun, thinking it would protect them from people in their rough Chicago neighborhood. What they didn't know then was that the only person they would need protection from was their father.

Cameron paused, closed his eyes, and said a quick prayer asking God's forgiveness.

Opening his eyes, Cameron saw his father's gun pointed at his upper chest. Ramon's hand shook uncontrollably.

Maybe it was best. Killing his father was something he couldn't live with anyway. Cameron held his gun, shaking with equal amounts of anger and fear that his mom and sister would be left unprotected.

Was it too late to save his family?

Superwoman's Child: Son of a Single Mother

Suitable for young adults

Run!

That one word screamed from every corner of his mind, but Sean Morris was too afraid to move.

Run!

As much as his mind said, "nothing is as bad as it seems," if Sean's suspicions were correct, things were *worse* than they seemed.

His rapidly pounding heart slammed against his chest. Sweat poured down his face. Fear gripped him in its ugly jaw. Memories of last year came flooding back with full clarity and with every vision his mind screamed . . . *Run!*

Although fright had kept his feet rooted to the floor of his bedroom, his legs finally had another idea—the right idea—*Run!*

Dashing out of his house into the icy winter night, the thirteen-year-old came to a frightening reality: his mother would probably kill him this time.

The last time she was this angry, she couldn't find the belt fast enough and had whipped him so hard that the bath brush imprint stayed on his butt, arms, and thighs for days. Whenever he was within her reach, the brush landed on some part of his body. That time he was just getting ready for bed and had run from the house butt-naked, bare feet trampling through six-foot snowdrifts. He barely felt the wind on his butt. He didn't bother cupping a hand over his exposed genitals as he ran the eight blocks to safety—Kevin's house. Kevin's mother had called Cynthia Morris, Sean's mother, and after a short conversation, Sean had stayed with them overnight.

He had been so frightened that when he got to school the next day, he couldn't open his mouth. He was too upset to concentrate on his work. It only took a few questions from the principal and Sean was spilling his guts: The one woman who had protected him from the effects of the cruel world had—somehow—scared the living daylights out of him.

He spent a few months at his Grandmother Cecilia's house while his mother calmed down and went through therapy. She hadn't put a hand on him since. Even before that, whippings weren't normal—a couple of taps with a belt once a year in the month before his birthday was all he could remember. Until last year.

Now, a year later, he was running again. At least this time he was wearing clothes. At least this time, she had given him a few seconds before she went off the deep end.

Run!

And the reason was so simple. Sean had messed up in school again—easy to fix, if he knew how. Teachers were calling all the time about his missing assignments and the way he acted in school—talking in class, walking out without permission, and fighting with the kids that messed with him, which were most of the guys in his class.

Sean couldn't care less about school. What he did care about was that his mother said in that sad, flat tone. "I can't take this anymore." Sean knew those words by heart. He knew *exactly* what they meant. She was about to give him a serious whipping—no words in the dictionary or anywhere else could even begin to describe it. Especially since something a bit more extreme happened this time. Everyone in the house could have died.

Run!

The week before the Fourth of July, his father had given him fireworks. Not the cute little sparkly kind. No, Roberto gave him the stuff that could take off an arm or two, or rearrange a person's face. Big bang stuff. His mother was never supposed to know. But that all changed when his dad never showed. A sour smell hovered through the house. Three weeks of repairmen, several searches of the two-story house, and days of keeping the windows open even on the frosty fall mornings didn't turn up the source.

Earlier that morning while Sean was at school, Aunt Denise's quick trip to his room to scoop up overripe laundry solved the mystery. She dumped out his hamper, and the fireworks rolled onto the floor; anger lit a fuse under his aunt, then she lit a fuse under Cynthia.

How was he supposed to know that keeping the hamper near the radiator would activate those things? They just started turning on the heat higher and he had forgotten all about them. Just like his dad had forgotten all about him—The Fourth had come and long gone with no sign of his father.

Then Cynthia received another phone call. And it was "that time of the month." Then the real fireworks began.

Run!

Sprinting up the street across Mrs. Allen's lawn, Sean almost tripped over the nativity scene. He paused a second, putting baby Jesus back in place, saying a prayer to the little guy, hoping he was watching Sean's back. Sean never looked back to see if his mother was coming. He couldn't afford the time. When Cynthia Morris was angry, that old girl could cover some serious ground—those extra fifty pounds didn't matter. He had seen her go from zero to twenty miles per hour in less than three seconds—and that was on a *slow* day.

Sean should have seen the signs. Normally, she would just talk to him. Normally, she would give him a chance to explain. Normally, she would try to help him figure things out. But he remembered last year when she hit the roof. Then she hit him. And hurt him. That's what he couldn't take.

Whoever said PMS was a myth had never experienced his mother's anger. He knew when she would be reasonable. And just like now, he knew when to get the heck out of Dodge. Usually he kept a calendar and spent the night with Grandma Cecilia, but somehow he'd slipped up.

Run!

God Does Answer Prayers

The beeping noise hummed under the sound of frantic voices. Consistent, like a dripping faucet, it wore on Steven's nerves.

What is that noise? Steven opened his eyes. People in green, blood-covered hospital suits stood over him with surgical tools, preparing to do something to his body, but he didn't know what. He could hear them faintly, and their faces were covered with bright white masks so he couldn't tell male from female, or doctor from nurse.

All he could really hear was that consistent beeping noise from the heart monitor. And then it happened. The beeps became slower, slower, sloooooower. His twelve-year-old heart was slowing by the second.

Steven still hadn't realized that, somehow, he could see everything perched from his spot right above the operating table. How did he get there?

"What are they doing?"

It looked like they were trying to save his life or something, but he wondered how that could be when he felt fine. "He's bleeding out. Get the clamps," one of the nurses yelled.

He scanned the room—green tiled walls, bright white lights, and extra surgical equipment stood near the bed where his body lay on the white sheets. A flutter of activity took place near the upper part of his body as nurses passed tools, followed quick commands, and overall moved in synchronization as though this entire act were a dance.

For some strange reason, they were still trying to save his life, but they actually walked straight past the "real" him. A glance to his left found his mother and father both crying behind a large plate-glass window. His father's face radiated shame, while his mother kept on banging on the glass, mouthing the words, "Save… him… please."

Who was she talking about? She couldn't have been talking about him. He was sitting up, feeling fine, and watching everything. Steven's face wrinkled in confusion, until one of the doctors lowered the window shade, blocking out the view of his parents. Steven slowly glanced behind him, and shock exploded from every corner of his mind. His own reflection glared back at him. He looked exactly like the Steven he remembered and, at the same time, looked nothing like the Steven he had been for twelve years.

Jumping further away from the table, he soon hovered in the upper corner of the room as questions whirled in his mind. How could that be me? I'm standing right here. It was painful to see himself lying on an emergency room table as doctors feverishly worked on his body, trying to get his heart back to a normal speed. Now he knew the reason for his parents' tears. But how did he get like this? How did Steven end up on that table?

Steven wasn't in a gang, so that couldn't have been it. There were no accidental shootings at school that day, so that was out of the question.

Steven was startled by the loud beeping sound, which suddenly switched from a beep to a flat, solid tone.

"He's flat lining. Get the paddles."

A nurse disappeared and a few seconds later, a loud bursting noise came from behind him. He turned around and quickly moved out of the way as a nurse rolled in the cart with electric shock paddles. The nurse splattered liquid on the paddles and placed them on his chest. "Clear." She paused, then added, "No pulse, Doctor."

"I need more. Give me three cc's of—"

Steven hovered there, witnessing how fast everything was flashing before his eyes. "Ouch, what the—" Although Steven wasn't connected to his body anymore, he could still feel the shock every time the jolt of electricity passed through his body. He also felt weak, as though he were fading, drifting away.

"Clear."

Steven lowered to the ground.

"We're losing him..." one of the nurses screamed.

What happened to me?

"Clear!"

Knight of Irondale

For 18 and up

Excerpt from Knight of Irondale
(Based on the real life experience)

Melissa Vidal pulled the phone away from her ear and put it on speakerphone. "Wait. What? Say that again."

"Ms. Vidal, the limo will be there tomorrow at six to pick Christian up for prom."

"Prom?" she locked a gaze on Christian, who sat straight up upon hearing that one word fall from her lips.

"Prom. Your son is taking my daughter to prom tomorrow night."

"Oh, he is, is he?" she said, putting a heated glare on him. "First I'm hearing of it."

Seventeen-year-old Christian grimaced and said a quick prayer.

"Well, I'm sorry to inform you," his mother said into the phone. "But young Mr. Vidal hasn't kept up with his schoolwork, so he can't go anywhere."

A sinking feeling hit the pit of Christian's belly at the thought of him not being able to keep his word.

"I truly apologize that no one thought to clue me in on things before now," Melissa said. "How on earth did it get this far along?"

"From what I understand, my daughter's friend at their Chicago Urban League class mentioned that my daughter didn't have a date for prom. Christian volunteered."

"Did he? Hmm…"

Christian sank into the sofa. Volunteering wasn't a hardship, since he'd had a pretty big crush on Neesha ever since Adam took that bite of the apple, then threw Eve under the bus during interrogation.

"Yes, and he came over to meet me and my husband and everything. He's such a charming young man."

"That he is," Melissa said, one eyebrow raised. "Charming. That he is."

"And they worked out the colors and outfits. He bought her a corsage—it's here already. The plan was to get dressed here and take off from my house."

"You don't say?" Her eyes shot daggers his way, and he tried to disappear into the cushion.

"You sound a little—pissed."

"Pissed. No, nothing like that," she countered. "Shocked, most definitely. I hate to disappoint your daughter, but young Mr. Vidal isn't able to go anywhere. He's been clowning on homework and assignments and isn't doing too well."

Silence on both ends ramped up his anxiety a notch or two.

"I can respect that," Ms. Carpenter said. "I'm not happy, but … I understand." She disconnected the call.

"Mama, please don't penalize Neesha because of me," Christian pleaded, getting to his feet and trying to find the words that would allow things to move forward.

"You should've thought of that before you went and landed yourself a whole prom experience without a word in my direction." She shook her finger at him. "You knew you were wrong. That's why you did it all secret-like. Bottom line."

True. But there was so much going on with him. So many doubts about why he wasn't enough for his father. He'd done everything, all the right things, and his father was still … absent. Like he never mattered. So much anger stirred in his soul that Christian stopped caring about much else—school, home, church. Doing this one small thing for Neesha had brought him some semblance of happiness.

"Mama, if I bring all of my work up to date and you get a call from my teachers …"

She thought about that for a long while, and an entire eternity passed before she answered, "Then you can go. But Christian, you're so far behind that I don't think you'll be able to make anything up." She dropped down into a seat at the kitchen table, picked up the newspaper and popped it open casually, like she hadn't imploded his entire teenage universe. "You're going to have another prom in a year. You can wait."

"But hers is tomorrow," he protested, a sinking feeling populating the pit of his belly. "I can't leave her hanging."

"But you can leave me hanging?" she snapped, and her hand slipped onto her fleshy hips. He knew he was all the way in trouble then. "And leave your education hanging, right? And you can leave your life hanging?"

Christian sighed, knowing she was right. He had let his anger with his father derail his life. And it wasn't affecting his father, it was directly affecting Christian. His father wouldn't even know any of this was happening. Christian needed to get his act together and fast. Not just for Neesha, but for himself.

"I want to keep my word," he said, resolved in what he had to do. "It's not about prom. It's about her."

"So now she's your girlfriend?"

"No, she's just a friend," he protested, but inwardly he was hoping for that to happen at some point. Neesha was amazing, smart, funny and beautiful. "But I do like her, and I came through when others didn't. Same way Dad didn't come through for you."

Her face was devoid of any emotion as she mulled that over. "You know you were dead wrong for that."

"Yes ma'am," he conceded.

Sadness clouded her features and he didn't feel good about being the one to put it there.

"I'm sorry for not telling you."

"But I need you to be just as diligent about your schoolwork as you are about making this prom thing happen." She placed a hand over his heart. "And I'm going to need you to let go of trying to get your father on board with being a father, because it's just not in him. You've been waiting all these years for him to show up in your life. You need to show up for your own self."

"Yes ma'am." He kissed her on the cheek and reached for his book bag. "I have to get in early. I have to hit up my teachers before class starts."

With that said, he was out the door.

That morning, Christian spoke with each one of his instructors and explained the situation. They gave him until the next morning to turn in all the assignments he had missed for the passing grade he needed, with a promise of additional work to bring his average from a C to an A within a week.

Christian didn't leave school until nine that night, then went home to finish, with eyelids drooping, deadlines approaching, and his mother keeping a watchful eye. She brought him a cup of coffee to keep him going. He didn't even like coffee, but he poured it down the hatch since it was going to keep him awake long enough to finish.

With completed assignments in hand, Christian was up again at the crack of dawn. He showered and was out the door, waiting in the school office for each instructor to arrive. He had never been so nervous in his entire life.

Over the course of that morning, they graded all of the work, and then called his mother—one by one—to inform her of his status. Only one required additional work at the last minute, throwing a little salt in the game, but by three o'clock, Christian was clear on their end.

Christian asked Principal Hawkins if he could use the phone to call Ms. Carpenter and let her know he would be able to take Neesha to the prom.

"With all due respect, Christian," Ms. Carpenter said in a sour tone when he got her on the phone. "I'm going to need to hear this directly from your mother."

Christian sighed, realizing he'd lost her trust. In that moment he promised to never put himself in a position where anyone would question his word again. "I understand. She's at work. I'll call her again now."

Reaching his mother seemed as though it took forever and two extra days. She agreed to call Neesha's mother and then call him back. Thirty minutes of waiting while reading another assignment, then both his mother and Ms. Carpenter were on a three-way call with Principal Hawkins.

At the end of the call, after accepting yet another apology from Christian, his mother agreed to let him escort Neesha to prom. Ms. Carpenter even told Christian's mother that she had much respect for how she had handled things."

Naleighna Kai is the *USA TODAY, Essence®* national bestselling and award-winning author of several women's fiction, contemporary fiction, Christian fiction, Romance, erotica, and science fiction novels that plumb the depth of unique relationships and women's issues. She is also a contributor to a *New York Times* bestseller, one of AALBC's 100 Top Authors, a member of CVS Hall of Fame, Mercedes Benz Mentor Award Nominee, and the E. Lynn Harris Author of Distinction.

In addition to successfully cracking the code of landing a deal for herself and others with a major publishing house, she continues to "pay it forward" by organizing the annual Cavalcade of Authors and NK's Tribe Called Success which gives readers intimate access to the most accomplished writing talent today. She also serves as CEO of The Macro Group, LLC which offers aspiring and established authors assistance with ghostwriting, developmental editing, publishing, marketing, and other services to jump-start or enhance their writing careers.

www.naleighnakai.com

FB: @naleighnakai
IG: @naleighnakai
TW: @naleighnakai

The Merry Hearts Inspirational Series will warm your heart and touch your soul...

www.ingramcontent.com/pod-product-compliance
Lightning Source LLC
Chambersburg PA
CBHW011803040426
42451CB00019B/3491